ALSO BY RACHEL HOLMES

Scanty Particulars

AFRICAN QUEEN

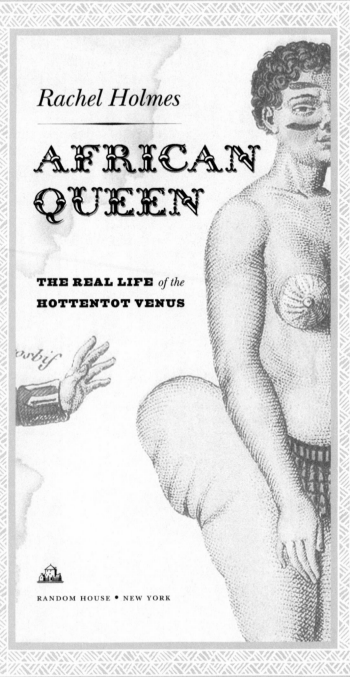

Rachel Holmes

AFRICAN QUEEN

THE REAL LIFE *of the* HOTTENTOT VENUS

RANDOM HOUSE • NEW YORK

Published in the United States by Random House, an imprint
of The Random House Publishing Group, a division
of Random House, Inc., New York.

RANDOM HOUSE and colophon are registered trademarks
of Random House, Inc.

Published in Great Britain by Bloomsbury Publishing plc, London.

Grateful acknowledgment is made to Diana Ferrus and WEAVE Collective
for permission to reprint eight lines from "I've come to take you
home—a tribute to Sarah Baartman" by Diana Ferrus, published in
*Ink@Boilingpoint: A Selection of 21st Century Black Women's Poetry from the Tip
of Africa* (Cape Town, South Africa: WEAVE Collective, 2002), 150.
Reprinted by permission of Diana Ferrus and WEAVE Collective.

Library of Congress Cataloging-in-Publication Data

Holmes, Rachel.
African queen: the real life of the Hottentot
Venus / Rachel Holmes.—1st ed.
p.   cm.
Includes bibliographical references.
ISBN 978-1-4000-6136-5
1. Baartman, Sarah.   2. Women, Khoikhoi—Biography.
3. Women, Khoikhoi—Europe—History—19th century.
4. Women, Khoikhoi—Europe—Social conditions.
5. Exploitation—Europe—History—19th century.   6. Racism in museum exhibits—Europe—History—19th century.   7. Museum exhibits—
Moral and ethical aspects—Europe.   I. Title.

DT1768.K56B34 2007
305.48'8961—dc22
[B]   2006045166

Printed in the United States of America on acid-free paper

www.atrandom.com

2 4 6 8 9 7 5 3

Book design by Simon M. Sullivan

For Jerry Brotton

And he said unto me, Son of man, can these bones live?
And I answered, O Lord God, thou knowest.
Ezekiel 37:3

The story of Sarah Baartman is the story of the
African people of our country in all their echelons.
President Thabo Mbeki

The rear end exists, I see no reason to be ashamed of it.
It's true that there are rear ends so stupid, so
pretentious, so insignificant, that they're
only good for sitting on.
Josephine Baker

I am a sex-o-matic Venus freak when I'm with you.
Macy Gray

CONTENTS

A NOTE ON NAMING

SAARTJIE BAARTMAN was born in South Africa in 1789. Her name is pronounced "Saar-key," with a roll on the *r*. *Saartjie* is an Afrikaans name and, like her surname, pure creole, the indigenous flowering of a name cross-fertilized by diverse languages and cultures. She may have been given a Khoisan name at birth, but it never entered written historical records. Throughout her short life she referred to herself as Saartjie.

Baartman, inherited from her father, means literally "bearded man." *Saartjie* translates into "Little Sara," but the intensity of meanings created by the *-tjie* suffix is lost in English. In Afrikaans, this suffix makes a diminutive of a noun. The construction derives from Dutch, in which the standard rule for creating a diminutive is to add *-tje* to a noun. Using the diminutive form of a name in Afrikaans has two different functions. It indicates smaller size, but it is also a powerful way of expressing sentiment. The key emotion expressed by the *-tjie* diminutive is endearment. Used between friends, family members, lovers, and equals of all classes and races, it is a verbal demonstration of affection and care.

However, because a diminutive reduces the size of what it names, the *-tjie* suffix has also been used to subordinate and enforce servitude. Deployed in historical contexts where one individual assumed power over another—white to black, master to servant, male to female—this verbal miniaturizing could express unequal power relations. During the colonial eras and apartheid, the *-tjie* suffix was often used by whites to indicate contempt, belittlement, and domination over black people. In the politically infused and blood-soaked history of language oppression in South Africa, to mark a person's name with a diminutive became, within this context, a racist speech act.

Saartjie Baartman is South Africa's most famous and revered national icon of the colonial era. As is usually the case with such iconic figures, there is some debate over her proper naming. Saartjie was known by several monikers during her lifetime, including the Christianized Sarah Bartmann.

Today the issue of her proper naming is divided between those who favor the Anglophone Sarah, or Sara, and those who think of her as Saartjie. To some, Sarah, or Sara, is a respectful honorific that distances her from the legacy of racism lingering in the diminutive applied to a tragic figure. For others, Saartjie is the fond evocation of her truest name, which emphasizes her South African heritage. Although sometimes bitterly debated, both positions share the recognition that naming is one of the profound forms of power.

Saartjie was her name in life as she lived it.

AFRICAN QUEEN

NOW EXHIBITING

AT

Nº 225, Piccadilly,

NEAR

THE TOP OF THE HAY-MARKET,

From TWELVE 'till FOUR o'Clock.

Admittance, 2s. each.

THE

Hottentot Venus,

JUST ARRIVED FROM THE

INTERIOR OF AFRICA;

THE GREATEST

PHŒNOMENON

Ever exhibited in this Country;

Whose Stay in the Metropolis will be but short.

SAARTJIE BAARTMAN, stage name the Hottentot Venus, emerged from behind a crimson velvet curtain, stepped out onto the three-foot-high stage in pointed green ribboned slippers, and surveyed her audience with a bold stare. Her high cheekbones and dramatic greasepaint and soot makeup gave her a prophetic, enigmatic look. Smoke coiled upwards from the pipe firmly gripped in the corner of her perfect Cupid's-bow mouth, drawing attention to her dimpled cheeks and heart-shaped face. It was a damp autumnal afternoon in London, 1810, and Saartjie was a long, long way from home.

Less than four feet, seven inches in height, she was a diminutive goddess. The springy pelt of her voluminous fur cloak draped from her shoulders to her feet, an African version of the corn gold tresses of Sandro Botticelli's Venus, and every inch of its luxuriant, labial, curled hair was equally suggestive.

Light and dark faces peered back up at her. Saartjie saw their eyes dilate with wonder, then narrow again speculatively, as if uncertain of how to evaluate the vision of an African Venus arising before them, out of the gleaming candlelight and fug of eye-watering smoke from the oil lamps that illuminated the auditorium. Framing Saartjie, the audience could see a small grass hut and painted boards depicting pastoral African scenery and verdant, exotic plants. According to the posters that advertised the recent arrival of the Hottentot Venus in blazing colors and huge printed letters all over central London, these settings depicted the mysterious interior of Africa—although where exactly that might be, many in the crowd were not sure.

To the audience that gazed up curiously at Saartjie, *Venus* was simply a synonym for sex; to behold the figure of Venus, or to hear her name, was to be prompted to think about lust, or love. At the same time, the word *Hottentot* signified all that was strange, disturbing, alien, and possibly, sexually deviant. Some, especially the elite viewers, had heard travelers' tales of mysterious Hottentot women, reputed to have enormous buttocks and strangely elongated labia, and to smoke a great deal. And here she was, a fantasy made flesh, tinted gold by the stage light, elevated above them, uniting the full imaginary force of these two powerful words: *Hottentot* and *Venus.* Her skintight, skin-colored body stocking clung to her so snugly that it was plain for all to see that she wore no corset, stockings, or drawers beneath. Most shockingly, the luminous ropes of ivory-colored ostrich eggshell beads that cascaded from her neck to her waist failed entirely to conceal her nipples, visible through the thin silken fabric.

The illuminated auditorium enabled Saartjie to see her audience almost as well as they could see her. She observed with great interest two men of distinctive appearance who entered the theater together and gazed up at her in rapt fascination. One was statuesque, hawk nosed, and haughty looking. The other was stocky, with curly hair and twisted features. Though Saartjie did not as yet know who they were, most of England did, and a murmur of recognition rippled through the crowd. The tall, grave-countenanced man was John Kemble, the nation's most famous actor, and the short man was comedian Charles Mathews, celebrated as the best stand-up comic and impersonator in the land.

Kemble stared fixedly at Saartjie, in a manner described in the folk stories of her childhood as being like a lion looking at the moon. He was just on the point of approaching the stage to address her, when suddenly a white woman elbowed forward, reached up, and coolly pinched her, very hard. Shocked, Saartjie stooped down to push her assailant away, but as she did so, another fashionable female in a high-waisted Empire topcoat (so beloved of Jane Austen heroines) clambered up onto the stage and poked her sharply in the buttocks with her furled parasol, drawling that "she wished to ascertain that all was . . . 'nattral.' " Before Saartjie had the opportunity to defend herself, a smartly dressed gentleman joined forces with her ungentle genteel aggressors, and prodded her with his walking cane.

The manager of the African Venus, Hendrik Cesars, jumped up onto the stage and declared the show over for the afternoon. As the crowd dispersed, Kemble, muttering "Poor, poor creature!" stalked up to Cesars and protested at the assaults on Saartjie, firing questions at him about her state of mind, comfort, and well-being. The actor vehemently declined the manager's wheedling, pacifying encouragements to touch her, objecting, "No, no, poor creature, no!"

Charles Mathews, who wrote up these events later in his diary, observed that Saartjie watched the exchange between Kemble and Cesars attentively. "She was," he said, "obviously very pleased; and, patting her hands together, and holding them up in evident admiration, uttered the unintelligible words, 'O ma Babba! O ma Babba!,' gazing at the tragedian with unequivocal delight." For a well-built woman, she had an unexpected daintiness and lightness in her gestures.

"What does she say, sir?" Kemble asked Cesars. "Does she call me her *papa*?"

"No, sir," the manager answered, "she says, you are a very fine man."

Saartjie's dignified response to Kemble was a classic expression of *ubuntu,* the African philosophy of humanity, fellow feeling, social decorum, and kindness. Her words signified respect and thanks, and clapping her hands was a courteous gesture of humility. Saartjie was offering appreciation to Kemble for his admiration and concern, and showing esteem for a man who, in her eyes, was a fatherly, and rather handsome, figure.

"Upon my word," Kemble retorted, emphatically inhaling a pinch of snuff, "the lady does me an infinite honour!"

The two entertainers left together. "Now Mathews, my good fellow, do you know this is a sight which makes me *mel*ancholy. I dare say, now, they ill-use that poor creature! Good God—how very shock-

ing!" Kemble and Mathews sauntered off down Piccadilly in search
of afternoon tea, speculating about Saartjie and her circumstances.
However, just like all the rest of the audience who had paid two
shillings to gape at the Hottentot Venus that afternoon, they knew almost nothing about her.

Saartjie was twenty-two years old. Six months previously, she had
arrived in England on a ship from the Cape Colony, with a British
military doctor named Alexander Dunlop, his South African manservant, Hendrik Cesars, and a former black slave now apprenticed as
Dunlop's servant. Saartjie lived with them in York Street, a short thoroughfare to the south of Piccadilly connecting Jermyn Street with St.
James's Square, and named in compliment to King James II.
Saartjie's new home was at the heart of London's most fashionable
district, and a world away from her previous life.

A MONTH PRIOR TO the visit that Mathews and Kemble paid to
Saartjie's show, on Wednesday September 12, Sir Joseph Banks, president of the Royal Society, received an invitation to attend an exclusive preview of the Hottentot Venus on the following Monday. This
private viewing was to be held nearby in "the house of exhibition" at
225 Piccadilly, and the invitation was from a man named Hendrik
Cesars. Banks discovered that similar invitations had been sent to scientists, naturalists, and fashionable members of high society, as well
as a variety of impresarios, including Richard Brinsley Sheridan, the
now-elderly playwright and politician, and William Bullock, famed
manager of the Liverpool Museum, London's bestselling attraction.
On Thursday September 20, three days after the preview, an advertisement using the same wording as the invitation appeared in the
Morning Herald and the *Morning Post,* announcing the opening of
London's latest curiosity to the public:

> The Hottentot Venus.—Just arrived, and may be seen between
> the hours of one and five o'clock in the afternoon, at No 225,
> Piccadilly, from the banks of the river Gamtoos, on the bor-
> ders of Kaffraria, in the interior of South Africa, a most cor-

rect and perfect specimen of that race of people. From this extraordinary phenomenon of nature, the Public will have an opportunity of judging how far she exceeds any description given by historians of that tribe of the human race. She is habited in the dress of her country, with all the rude ornaments usually worn by those people. She has been seen by the principal Literati in this Metropolis, who were all greatly astonished, as well as highly gratified, with the sight of so wonderful a specimen of the human race. She has been brought to this country at a considerable expense by Hendrik Cesars, a native of the Cape, and their stay will be but short. To commence on Monday, the 24th instant.—Admittance 2s each.

This hyperbolical advertisement, promising so much, in fact told very little. Yet it heralded the opening of London's most famous and controversial theatrical phenomenon of the winter of 1810. Almost overnight, the Hottentot Venus became the sensation of the metropolis, both onstage and off. Who was she, and where did she come from? And how did this young black woman who sang, danced, and played the guitar come to be upon the London stage, got up like a fetish and performing like a showgirl?

Chapter 2

M TAI !NUERRE—

"MY MOTHER'S COUNTRY"

$\mathcal{S}$AARTJIE BAARTMAN WAS BORN in 1789 in the Gamtoos River Valley, a lushly forested, semitropical estuary on the bitterly contested eastern frontier of the Cape Colony. Although Africa and Europe were worlds apart, the repercussions of that revolutionary year in Europe had a definitive impact on Saartjie's childhood.

She did not remember her mother, who died before Saartjie had reached her first birthday. Lastborn, she had four brothers and two sisters, who probably became responsible for her care. If she had substitute mothers—grandmother, stepmother, or aunt—she never mentioned them. Saartjie's father, the dominant influence on her childhood, was a cattle drover and hunter, a late-eighteenth-century South African frontier cowboy.

The hills and forests of Saartjie's homeland were filled with elephants, hunters' guns, and Christian missionaries. Lions were a constant threat. Saartjie grew up much exposed to the elements. Summers were hot and humid; winters slightly milder. Rains dampened the firewood that Saartjie and her sisters carried home on their heads. Burning winds intensified the summer heat, blew cold in the winter, but never seemed to blow away the all-pervasive dust that got into everything: nostrils, ears, cooking pots of maize porridge and meat stew, and the straw thatching of the one-room shack in which all the Baartman family lived.

The Gamtoos flows from the confluence of the Kouga and Groot rivers through green lagoons to the ocean. In Saartjie's day, tall bush fringed the riverbanks and coastline. Lowland plains shelved towards the interior, deep valleys of thorn trees and open bushveld stretched between rocky escarpments and gorges. Visible for miles, the high hills were covered so densely with thickets of flame red and orange aloes that when they flowered, the landscape looked ablaze.

Although palm fringed and fertile, Saartjie's homeland was no Edenic pastoral idyll: it was a war zone. Until the arrival of the European colonists at the Cape in the seventeenth century, the Gamtoos region was untroubled by Christian God or European law. However, by the time of Saartjie's infancy the eastern frontier had become a scene of bloody contest between indigenous and colonial groups. Saartjie's people, the Khoisan, were at the epicenter of this bitter struggle.

Saartjie was descended from the Eastern Cape Khoisan, the long-intermingled society of herding, pastoralist Khoekhoen (Khoi) and hunter-gatherer, nomadic San, native to South Africa since prehistoric times. Saartjie's ancestors named the Gamtoos; many rivers, mountains, deserts, animals, and plants in the region today still bear Khoisan names.

In the seventeenth century, the Cape Khoisan clans were numerous, cattle-rich, and autonomous, but by the last decades of the eighteenth century, their wealth was all but annihilated. When the Europeans arrived, they had Bibles and the Khoisan had land. By the time of Saartjie's birth, the Khoisan had the Bibles, and the Europeans had most of the land. For more than a hundred and fifty years the Western Cape Khoisan prevented seafaring European invaders from establishing a foothold in South Africa. From the first Portuguese landing, in 1488, they held off the Portuguese, Dutch, English, and French. Finally, in 1652, the Dutch East India Company (VOC) established the first permanent settlement, a refreshment station in Table Bay, with Governor Jan van Riebeeck at the helm.

The Europeans forging a trading seaway to the east struggled, and failed, to master the Khoisan languages, particularly their complex phonology of implosive consonants, or "clicks." The tongue-tied Europeans dubbed the Khoekhoen "Hottentots," and the San "Bushmen." Europeans initially regarded the cattle-propertied Hottentots as trading partners, diplomatic and cultural go-betweens, and potential employees. The Bushmen, on the other hand, with their ability to live from the "bush" and their lack of livestock, seemed elusive, unassimilable, and insubordinate to a European value system of private property ownership and fixed settlement. But in the end any distinctive cultural identity was construed as negative and inferior, and thus as a justification for conquest. Van Riebeeck's opinion that Hottentots were "a dull, stupid, lazy, stinking nation," who were "bold thievish and not to be trusted," was long representative of the dominant European view of Khoisan people.

In the racial thinking of the nineteenth century, the economic and social differences between the Khoi and the San were transposed into differences of ethnic origin. Over time, colonizers forced an association between "Hottentots" and servility; "Bushmen" and resistance. These divisions allowed the invading Europeans to make distinctions between "good" (tractable) and "bad" (resistant) natives, in order to subordinate the Khoisan and repress their long history of armed struggle.

During the eighteenth century the Eastern Cape Khoisan were squeezed into an ever-narrowing corridor of their ancestral lands by advancing settler-colonists. From the west came Europeans: traders, hunters, travelers, missionaries, and cattle farmers. Also from the west came the Western Cape Khoisan, poor trekboers, and colonial dissidents driven away from the Dutch settlements due to intermarriage or illegitimacy. These latter groups were people of diverse ethnic origins, whose ancestry bonded together slaves from Africa and Malaysia with white Europeans of all classes. From the east came the Xhosa, pushing westwards along the coast in search of new grazing and farm lands. Many of the Eastern Cape Khoisan lived among the Xhosa, a legacy of the ancient trading routes that looped through the region.

A semiautonomous community of Eastern Cape Khoisan, Saartjie's family among them, continued to live on their traditional grazing lands at the mouth of the Gamtoos. However, as their cattle stocks dwindled, they became increasingly dependent on wage labor, especially on the three farms surrounding them. In 1778 Saartjie's people were dispossessed when the government "loaned" these farms to a Dutch farmer, Hilgert Muller. Muller and his henchmen went on a murderous landgrab; they ignored established grazing rights, stole cattle, drove people from their homes, and raped and captured women and children, forcing them into concubinage and domestic service. The Gamtoos Khoisan were either compelled to work for the colonists, or organized themselves into units of armed resistance, instigating cattle raids to regain their stock.

From infancy, Saartjie grew up amid a mixed community of Khoisan, Xhosa, Europeans, and slaves who were settled down very close to one another. Most Xhosa farmers were more established, and wealthier in both cattle and culture, than the vagrant, shoeless Dutch trekboers. Saartjie did not go to school, and never learned to read or write. She grew up speaking Afrikaans and possibly some Khoisan and Xhosa. Someone taught Saartjie to play music at an early age. She mastered the *ramkie*, a forerunner to the tin-can guitar, adapted specifically to blend Khoisan and Western folk songs. She was also adept on the single-string violin, or *mamokhorong*, important in Khoisan music traditions involving dancing, and notoriously tricky to master.

Because livestock ownership was central to their culture, the Khoisan were expert herders and cattlemen. This made them desirable employees for Xhosa and Dutch farmers, for whom they worked as a means to try and rebuild their own depleted herds. The Khoisan had legendary abilities as horsemen and marksmen, and were highly prized war allies. Skilled cattlemen like Saartjie's father periodically served the Dutch East India Company, working to provision the Cape Colony. In harvest season some of them hired themselves out to the farmers for a fixed fee. Otherwise, they herded cattle, drove wagons, or acted as hunting guides; they were paid in tobacco, cheap wine, and sheep. The few head of livestock the Khoisan owned roamed long communal pastures, but grazing rights on land settled by white farmers became increasingly disputed.

On horseback, Saartjie's father must have looked imposing to his tiny daughter. He was a large figure in her world, who comforted and provided for her, but was, from economic necessity, so often absent. She explained in later life that he was "in the habit of going with Cattle from the interior to the Cape." This was a 930-mile round trip, and Baartman was away for long periods, returning with intriguing travel stories for his children.

Throughout Saartjie's childhood the hills of the Gamtoos were filled with gunfire, smoke, and fear. The so-called Bushman Wars had escalated to an unprecedented level of ferocity. The Khoisan were pressured on all sides. Boer commando raids deepened in horror and magnitude. The frontier ignited into widespread violence, with the Khoisan ranks joined by escaped slaves, white deserters, and Khoi servants. The rape and capture of children who would be forced to work as servants exacerbated the conflict. Terrible atrocities often took place in these raids, including the violent murder of infants "too young to be carried by the farmers for the purpose to use them as bondsmen." Entrapped Khoisan children were commonly sold, in exchange for a horse, gun, or pair of shoes. Body parts were kept as trophies by Europeans.

When Saartjie was six years old, the British arrived, prompted by events in Napoleonic Europe. In the aftermath of the French Revolution, the French republican armies helped the Dutch republican party establish the Batavian Republic in Holland. Prince William and supporters of the House of Orange fled to monarchist-friendly England, and persuaded the government to take territorial possession of the Cape Colony in order to prevent it from falling into republican French hands. In September 1795, following two months of fighting, the Dutch governor surrendered the colony to the British.

Seizing the rhetoric of pro-French Jacobinism, the Dutch settlers rebelled against the occupation, and from 1795 to 1799 waged war on the British, determined to establish their own Boer republic in support of the Batavian regime. The British allied themselves with the Xhosa and Khoisan, promising to restore their livestock and land and to release the Khoisan from servitude to the Dutch settlers. Many Gamtoos Khoisan cattlemen fought as mounted riflemen in the quashing of the Boer rebellion, and probably Saartjie's father was among them.

In 1799 the Khoisan and Xhosa militias defeated the Dutch, at which point their British allies promptly reneged on their promises, attempted to force the Xhosa back eastwards, and ignored Khoisan claims for land rights and autonomy. Furious at this duplicitous betrayal, the Xhosa and Khoisan regrouped into fighting units, determined to drive the British out of the eastern frontier. The British turned to their former Dutch enemies for assistance. For the colonists, this third frontier war of 1799–1802 was the most bloody and disastrous. The British and Dutch had armed the Xhosa and Khoisan themselves, by selling them weapons in exchange for cattle. Through diverse alliances and successive wars, the Khoisan, Xhosa, runaway slaves, and dissident whites of the eastern frontier sustained a long campaign of opposition to the colonial conquest of South Africa throughout the nineteenth century.

Stock theft in retaliation against settler encroachment was unrelenting. The Khoisan were dangerous foes, feared equally by the Xhosa and by whites. Run ragged by stock theft and obligatory military service, many squatting white farmers were driven from the land. Simultaneously, pitted against each other by trade wars and desperation, the Khoisan raided their own neighbors.

These were the bewildering and terrifying events that shaped the landscape of Saartjie's upbringing. Amid all the grand open vistas of the veld, the shady forests, long beaches, and vaulted skies, children like Saartjie lived in the line of fire in a raw, frontier, intimately communal, hand-to-mouth existence.

In 1807, when she was seventeen or eighteen, Saartjie's father was murdered. In 1810 she said her father had been killed on one of his frequent cattle runs to the Cape. Baartman was, in Saartjie's words, "killed by the 'Bosjemen' " during a skirmish with a "barbaric" European-led commando unit. Intended to supply the Cape and enrich its colonial farmers, cattle runs were a prime target for many warring factions, and it was almost impossible to distinguish between trading and commando raiding operations. However, the records describing Saartjie's accounts of the deaths of her father and mother are contradictory. Later, in 1815, an ailing, world-weary, and champagne-drunk Saartjie told a quite different story of her father's death and her separation from her family to an equally inebriated Dutch-speaking French journalist.

"My father," she explained, "was at the head of the hunters and my mother was the woman who organised the celebrations. Everyone sought to ally themselves with them, and I was greatly in demand." From among her many suitors, a young man named Solkar was the one who "entered most deeply" into her heart. Saartjie's parents arranged a feast to celebrate their daughter's forthcoming marriage, and for a betrothal gift, Solkar gave Saartjie a tortoiseshell pendant.

The festivities lengthened into sunset: "[T]he fires were lit on the hilltop. It was these very fires that betrayed us. We heard cries in the distance. We saw barbaric Europeans, and already in the midst of them were women struggling and refusing to follow in their foot-steps." Saartjie and Solkar's betrothal party had fallen prey to a rov-ing commando. Rifle shot blasted away the guitar, *goura*, and reed flute melodies. The men, led by the ardent young Solkar, threw themselves into battle against the commando raid.

The impassive sun returned in the morning, dispersing the cordite- and sulfur-imbued mist. It revealed an abandoned hilltop, where spilt human blood congealed with the fat of roasted meat and the ash of trampled fires. Saartjie's father and her lover Solkar were dead. Overnight, her childhood was stolen. She had been captured, taken by the commando, and forced, on foot, towards Cape Town.

At this point in her narrative, Saartjie kissed her tortoiseshell pen-dant and exclaimed, "[A]ll our defenders, our brothers, our lovers, all perished, and we unfortunate victims who did not die were tightly bound, and were taken away by the evildoers, far from our beloved forests, and driven, with a thousand insults, onto floating trees, where we saw nothing but the sea and the clouds."

Saartjie wore this tortoiseshell pendant round her neck for the rest of her life. This talisman is also recorded in the memory of a ges-ture, an etching in air. When subjected to the stress of public scrutiny by strangers, and at times of extreme vulnerability, Saartjie had an unconscious habit of repeatedly touching the pendant, "which she often took in her two hands, pressing it hard against her lips and lifting her eyes to heaven."

Saartjie was orphaned, female, and unprotected. In what can only be imagined as the most distressing circumstances, she was wrenched from her home, separated from her remaining family, and taken into the custody of a hunter and trader named Pieter Willem Cesars, a free black (*vryswarte*) from Cape Town. How Pieter Cesars came into Saartjie's life, she never explained, nor has it yet been discovered.

The fact that Saartjie had reached puberty may have saved her life. Pieter Cesars's brother and sister-in-law were adopting a child and needed a wet nurse, an unusual luxury for their class. Pieter Cesars decided to take Saartjie to the capital to become nursemaid to his soon-to-be adopted niece. Whether Pieter Cesars was Saartjie's captor or her savior remains one of the unsolved mysteries of her life. Hunters and traders were frequently involved in child catching in order to sell the children into service. Saartjie caught Pieter Cesars's attention; she was a good age for a nursemaid, and a sharp and strikingly pretty youngster. By taking Saartjie into service in his family Pieter Cesars may have, albeit inadvertently, saved her from a worse fate, such as being murdered during the raid or indentured to one of the local white-settler farms. For Saartjie, however, such distinctions between capture or delivery might have seemed largely irrelevant.

The murder of her father was the defining event of Saartjie's youth. Henceforward, the wishes of men dominated her life, because they held her in the grip of their economic and social power. Saartjie's relationship with paternalistic figures was shadowed by her unresolved attachment to an idealized father, snatched from her at the point she most needed and respected him, and before she had cause to rebel against him.

Even at this tender age, Saartjie already had more knowledge than many better-educated children. She had witnessed the relentless resistance of her people to conquest. She encountered ruthless prejudice based upon bigoted notions about the inherent passivity, servility, and inferiority of "Hottentots." However, Saartjie knew very well from personal experience that she was not the child of a passive people.

Saartjie's upbringing was conditioned by opposition and conflict, but she had also witnessed compromise and collaboration as responses to trade inducements, aggression, and war. Her childhood was therefore an intimate education in the fine balance between the risks of resistance and the compromises of survival.

Chapter 3
CITY OF LOST CHILDREN

$\mathcal{S}$AARTJIE LEFT THE HILLS of flaming poker-red aloes with Pieter Cesars and trekked overland some five hundred miles through the Breede River Valley and the Klein Karoo towards the great craggy ridge of the Hottentots Holland, the mountainous gateway between the south coast of Africa and the Cape Peninsula. Pieter hunted and called at small settlements and trading posts along the way. To Saartjie, the month-long journey must have seemed interminable.

They skirted thick, wooded mountains and tree-filled kloofs draped in knotty monkey ropes. At night, the bright four-star Southern Cross bisected the indigo sky. Finally, they arrived at the Cape Peninsula, meeting point of two oceans. For Saartjie, Cape Town was a new cosmopolitan world set in a sea of botanical green. The city was encircled by the giant's sweep of the Drakenstein mountains, culminating in the brooding, granite-purple Table Mountain and its buttressed escarpments forming the great, sweeping amphitheater of the Table Valley. Filled with sails, Cape Town harbor was a jostling commotion of chandlery and the brisk traffic of fishing schooners, brigs, barks, fully rigged tall ships, warships, and East Indiamen.

Saartjie had never before experienced humanity on such a scale. Cape Town's bustling hospitality prompted Captain James Cook to describe it as "one great Inn fitted up for the reception of all comers and goers." Saartjie, however, had come to Cape Town not to be waited on, but to serve. Clearly, Pieter trusted that Saartjie could be tried out as a nursemaid, a position well suited to a teenage girl.

There was also about her something very appealing. Although very small, she had an air of compact-limbed strength and watchful composure.

Pieter took Saartjie to his brother's home, "not 2 miles from the Cape," in the Table Valley: the place was later sketched by the missionary John Campbell as he passed by in 1815. Campbell annotated his drawing as the "House from which the Female in Piccadilly called the Hottentot Venus was taken," but failed to note its specific location. The sketch depicts a small flat-roofed Malay-style whitewashed stone cottage with the Moorish, Mediterranean appearance typical of the region. Attached to the side of the Cesars home were two *pondoks,* low-walled lean-to extensions with a single sloping roof, providing rudimentary slave quarters for their two domestic male slaves (*lyf-eigen-slaven*). The cottage had a wooden door, internal shutters on the windows, and a chimney in the kitchen, which was the heart of the house.

Saartjie became live-in "nursery maid" to Hendrik and Anna Catharina's newly adopted daughter, also called Anna Catharina. The specific terms of her employment are not recorded. Until 1809, there was no legal wage structure for Khoisan domestic servants, and they were usually absorbed into the household, working for food and shelter only. Female servants and slaves slept in the kitchen by the hearth, while male servants and slaves slept in outbuildings.

Hendrik Cesars and Anna Catharina Staal, "both born in this remote corner," had married in 1805. The will they drew up shortly after their wedding shows they expected to raise children. However, there was a medical problem, and within two years the couple applied to the governors of the Orphan Chamber to adopt a free child. The law of matrilineal descent, which applied to both free burghers and slaves, meant that Anna Catharina could pass her free-black status only to her natural-born offspring, or adopt a freeborn child from the Cape Town Orphan Chamber, which had been founded in the seventeenth century to protect the needs and interests of freeborn parentless children. (There was no provision for slave orphans until 1815.) Like Saartjie, little Anna Catharina was an orphan, a common tragedy in Cape Town, which slavery had made a city of lost children.

THE 1807 ABOLITION OF THE SLAVE TRADE ACT abolished the slave trade in all British colonies and made it illegal to carry slaves in British ships, but existing slaves remained the property of their owners for life, and their owners could still dispense their futures as they saw fit. The census of 1807, ordered to make an official count of the number of slaves in the colony at the time of abolition, recorded that Hendrik and Anna owned two male life-slaves over the age of sixteen, but kept no female slaves. They also had three male Khoisan servants over sixteen, and two female Khoisan servants over fourteen (described in the registers as "Hottentot, *in dienst*": in service, or indentured). Saartjie was one of these "indentured Hottentots."

The free blacks were the most urbanized and poorest of all slave owners, making their slave-owning behavior substantially different from other, richer groups. Hendrik was an illiterate manservant, employed by a British Army medical officer named Alexander Dunlop, staff surgeon to the Thirty-eighth Regiment of Foot and chief surgeon of the Slave Lodge. Cesars, or Cezars, from Caesar, is a name rooted in Romance rather than Germanic languages. South African genealogies list no Cesarses, in any variation of spelling, among the European South African settler families. However, Caesar, Cesar, and Cezars were very common slave names at the Cape from the 1700s. Anna Catharina, who was literate, was probably related to the Staals of Amsterdam who immigrated to the Cape in the eighteenth century.

The 1807 census registered Hendrik and Anna Catharina as free blacks. Legally, the term covered three main subgroups of the burghers. All liberated (manumitted) slaves entered the free-black community, but not all free blacks were descended from slaves. A significant proportion came from the population of convicts (mostly Indo-Chinese, Indonesian, or Sinhalese) and political exiles (predominantly Indonesian, many royalty or high-born) transported to the Cape. Among the prisoners of war brought to Cape Town, and frequently imprisoned for life on Robben Island, were priests and princes of Muslim states subverted or overthrown by the Dutch East India Company. The remaining population comprised ex-slaves and locally born free blacks—third, second, or first generation—descended from interracial unions.

Saartjie's overcrowded mixed household was a microcosm of the diversity of Cape Town. She was about eighteen when Pieter brought her to the city. However, even if she had been a minor there would have been no government record of her transfer to the Cesarses' employ, because there was no formal process for registering orphaned Khoisan or slave children. In the eyes of the law, they did not exist.

The legal technicalities that distinguished enserfed dependent from human chattel had a direct personal impact on Saartjie. Economically, sexually, and racially, she was unfree. However, her arrival in Cape Town coincided with the transition of the colony from Dutch republican to British rule, and with the changes in legislation and the slave trade that accompanied that shift.

Saartjie's duties revolved around taking care of little Anna Catharina, as well as domestic labor—washing, cleaning, and assisting with the cooking. It was common practice for Cape settler women to use female slaves as wet nurses for their infants, in order to increase their own fertility; but it was unusual for poorer families to employ a nursemaid to suckle their infants. Saartjie, however, could not have been a wet nurse without a baby of her own.

Due to the free-black status of her employers, Saartjie's social world was more permeable than it would have been were she entailed to a higher-class, white-settler family. Initially, her social life was an extension of her domestic responsibilities; snatched moments of liberty when running errands, and looking after little Anna Catharina and Pieter Cesars's three motherless sons on Sundays when the whole household attended church. These religious services provided one of her first opportunities to make acquaintances and friends.

Other intriguing opportunities for a teenager recently arrived from the provinces were provided by the taverns, inns, alehouses, and shebeens clustered around the harbor and tucked into every street of the expanding city. Hendrik's master, Alexander Dunlop, regarded by his fellow officers as a talented but renegade miscreant, was an exuberant frequenter of the tippling houses, known for his love of carousing with his social inferiors, particularly his manservant Hendrik.

Tavern nightlife was Saartjie's first small space of freedom. Her ability to play, sing, and dance made her popular. Sailors and the poorer servants of empire filled these taphouses, bringing with them sea shanties and folk songs that were blended with Khoisan and slave music traditions. During her first year in Cape Town, Saartjie fell for a young soldier whom she met, possibly, in church or at a tavern. His name is lost, but the resonant echo of a drumbeat locates Saartjie's lover as a regimental drummer attached to the Cape Town garrison.

Saartjie's drummer had musicality and boyish charm all wrapped in the alluring package of a soldier in uniform. British Army drummers traditionally had showy, distinctive dress and battle uniforms. In addition to their military duties, regimental musicians officiated at formal civil functions and featured among Cape Town's popular entertainers. Military musicians were much in demand in church and at weddings, parties, and taverns. In the egalitarian atmosphere of the multiracial shebeens the poorer classes of many continents rubbed shoulders, playing together and adapting their instruments. Sharing diverse musical traditions from Africa, the east, and Europe, they forged the foundations of the musical fusion that has become Cape Town's unique sound.

The encounter between Saartjie and her drummer boy quickly developed beyond high-spirited nights in the smoke-filled shebeens. The couple soon contrived to live together, despite their modest means. Saartjie moved in with her new lover. The British Army regiments were garrisoned at Cape Town Castle, and in a large barracks located a block north of the Parade. By tradition, girlfriends, prostitutes, and wives shared quarters with their men. Lowly drummers were billeted in dormitory barracks, where rough blanket dividers provided the only privacy for intimacy.

Saartjie continued to work for Hendrik and Anna, although she lost the benefits of being a live-in servant. The drummer's monthly wage sufficed for them both, although war-related inflation made the city expensive. His duty to wake up the regiment ensured that Saartjie could rise early and get to work on time.

Little is known about Saartjie's drummer. According to the London *Morning Herald,* he was Irish. Napoleon's surgeon Georges Cuvier claimed that Saartjie "said that she had been married to a Negro." It is possible that Saartjie's lover may have been a local Khoisan boy in the Cape Regiment, or an Nguni volunteer. There had been indigenous regiments attached to the Dutch and then British services since the eighteenth century. The Hottentot regiments, or Pandours, as they had previously been known, included mounted riflemen and light infantry; in 1806, after they had assisted the British to regain the Cape, these regiments were disbanded and absorbed into the regular British service. It is equally possible that Saartjie's drummer was West Indian, or a former slave posted to the drums in exchange for the promise of freedom. From the fourteenth century, there were black musicians and percussionists in the British Army. In the eighteenth century it was the fashion among many regiments to employ drummers from Africa and the West Indies. Black Guardsmen were familiar figures to early-nineteenth-century Londoners, having been part of the daily ceremony of the Changing of the Guard since the time of the Court of St. James.

In Cape Town, Saartjie first encountered the flavors of Napoleonic Europe. Watched with admiration by his new girlfriend, the drummer played in military parades attended by the privileged echelons of a European society very different from the ordinary foot soldiers of empire Saartjie encountered in the taverns. On her soldier's arm, Saartjie observed from the sidelines as the vanity fair of moneyed white society paraded the streets, and promenaded in the manicured Company Gardens at the heart of the city. William Jones, a young soldier stationed at the Cape, remarked on the manners and fashions of Georgian Cape Town:

The Company's Gardens are quite the Kensington of the place, the Ladies and Gentlemen walk there every evening after the sun is down; and it only wants lamps to make you imagine yourself near London. If Ostrich feathers can make Ladies fine, here they are in perfection.

The pleasures shared between Saartjie and her drummer soon led to their conventional outcome when, in 1807, she realized that she was pregnant. The pregnancy was successful, and, less conventionally, her young soldier took responsibility for the child. For two years, Saartjie had a new family. It was during this period that she wet-nursed Anna Catharina Cesars, following the common practice of Khoisan and slave nursemaids breast-feeding first their own child and then their employers' without a break, so that their milk did not dry up. Hendrik and Anna's need for a wet nurse gave them reason to encourage Saartjie's relationship with the drummer, and to support the birth of her child.

Then tragedy again struck Saartjie's life. Just before his or her second birthday, Saartjie's infant became desperately ill. Since Hendrik's employer, Alexander Dunlop, was chief surgeon of the Slave Lodge, where Khoisan patients were treated, it is likely that Hendrik asked his master to treat Saartjie's firstborn. But to no avail. "The child is since dead" was Saartjie's choked, stark epitaph to this irreparable loss. Yet again, family had been snatched from her. There is no record of the name or sex of Saartjie's baby, or why she or he died, and the commonest causes of Khoisan infant mortality in Cape Town during this period were not documented.

How different Saartjie's life might have been had her child lived. Her relationship did not withstand this calamity. It is unclear whether the drummer left Saartjie, or she him. For the short term, they had a fun, and seemingly loving, interlude. But an itinerant drummer boy had very little that a girl could count on for the long term. Or perhaps they could not adequately console each other for their baby's death. Following their bereavement, the drummer disappeared from Saartjie's life, and from the historical record. With this triple blow, Saartjie lost her firstborn, her lover, and the family she had sought to rebuild.

Saartjie was once again in a precarious position. Her livelihood depended upon her ability to wet-nurse Anna Catharina, and on her drummer's wages. Aged twenty-one, Saartjie was uncertain of her future value to the Cesarses, and her survival hung in the balance.

Chapter 4

STOWAWAY

BY THE END OF 1809 Saartjie's life had narrowed once again to domestic drudgery. The Cesarses kept her on as nursemaid, and she moved back into their cottage. While grieving for her own child, Saartjie had to continue to look after little Anna Catharina. It seemed increasingly that her value lay in her body, and the services it could provide for others.

Two unrelated events in 1809 catalyzed Saartjie's future. The first was the issuing of the new Hottentot Proclamation by the colonial government. The second was that Hendrik's master, Alexander Dunlop, on whom the Cesars household depended, lost his job.

The Hottentot Proclamation was issued by the Earl of Caledon, third British Governor of the Cape. This notorious piece of colonial legislation for the first time permitted the Khoisan to be legally indentured. The measure attempted, and failed, to address two irreconcilable problems. The colony had a labor shortage, exacerbated by the abolition of the slave trade in 1808. Simultaneously, missionaries protested the Khoisan's social and economic conditions, and argued for improvements in their judicial status. Inevitably, the effects of the Hottentot Proclamation proved contradictory. It tried to improve the legal status of the Khoisan by including them under the rule of law, but in order to do so, it introduced draconian constraints on their movement, and gave white masters unprecedented legal control over their Khoisan servants.

Hendrik and Anna Catharina were now required to officially register all the Khoisan members of their household. In compliance with the proclamation, Saartjie was taken before a magistrate and formally indentured as a "Hottentot" servant. Technically, Saartjie's formal registration as a servant entitled her to a wage and some basic conditions of employment. In reality, the government put little effort into monitoring the now "protected" interests of the Khoisan. In the revealing words of his Hottentot Proclamation, the Prospero-like Lord Caledon "extend[ed] his peculiar protection in nature of a guardian over the Hottentot nation under his government, by reason of their general imbecile state." Saartjie was now more vulnerable to exploitation, and subject to the authority of an absolute paternalism allegedly designed to protect her welfare.

During the same year that Saartjie's child died, Dunlop had been pitched headlong into a professional crisis. He lived in bachelor's lodgings in central Cape Town at 28 Wale Street, next door to the Slave Lodge. Dunlop had joined the Thirty-eighth Regiment of Foot as surgeon's mate in January 1792, was gazetted surgeon in August 1796, and became a staff surgeon in August 1803. In 1806, when the British captured the Cape, he was appointed military staff surgeon at the army General Hospital in Cape Town, and simultaneously was given the civil office of chief surgeon of the Slave Lodge, which since 1685 had provided medical treatment for slaves, Khoisan, prostitutes, and other groups excluded from care in the civil and military hospitals. The Slave Lodge was overcrowded, in urgent need of repair, and woefully short of resources.

Dunlop had a reputation for considerable skill as a physician, but he was undiplomatic to his ranked superiors and was well known for courting controversy. In 1809 Dunlop got embroiled in a dispute with the colonial authorities over the treatment of sick Khoisan women at the Slave Lodge. From the beginning of the British occupation, all sick Khoisan were referred to the Slave Lodge hospital, but there was no provision for treating women with venereal illnesses. In 1808, there was an alarming increase in the spread of sexually transmitted diseases among the troops, convicts, prisoners, and prison guards. Prostitutes were blamed, and Khoisan women singled out for particular censure. Dunlop and Dr. Hussey (inspector of hospitals and chief of the General Hospital) highlighted the need to treat "diseased Hottentot Women," and urged the government to take measures to separate them from the troops.

However, the administration procrastinated, and in return for inaction got a venereal epidemic. Finally, on April 1, 1809, the women were separated from the troops and sent to the slave hospital, under Dunlop's responsibility. The administration committed itself to covering the new costs for their treatment, but two months later Dunlop had yet to receive the additional grant. He raised the matter with the governor's office, requesting "such allowance as you may think proper for the medical care of those people." In January 1810, Dunlop submitted a total claim for 305 rix-dollars—a very large sum of money.

However, the parsimonious British government refused to pay, and ruled "any charge whatever with regard to Venereal Female Hottentots as altogether inadmissible." Dunlop, they stated, had willfully misunderstood his instructions.

Dunlop's vociferous protests provoked General Grey to complain about his conduct directly to Lord Caledon, and to beg the governor not to "pay one sixpence of the bill." Dunlop received a strong reprimand, and General Grey threatened that "if he gives further trouble I shall name another medical officer to his situation." Give further trouble is exactly what Dunlop did. Within the month he was placed on transfer back to England, and General Grey was looking for a replacement for both of his posts.

With Dunlop between jobs, Hendrik's future was uncertain, and with it the security of the Cesars family and its dependents. Having earned the disapproval of Lord Caledon and the military authorities, Dunlop had no option but to return to England and await a new posting. With his master leaving the Cape, Hendrik was out of a job. In all, the livelihoods of ten people, including Saartjie, depended upon Hendrik's employment.

Dunlop, Hendrik, and his brother Pieter must have been paying close attention to Saartjie, for it was at this point that they hatched an audacious plan. Looking for a means to secure a new livelihood,

Dunlop persuaded the Cesars brothers that Saartjie had lucrative potential as a scientific curiosity in England. In an African context Saartjie's build was unremarkable, but Dunlop believed that unfamiliarity could make her extraordinary in European eyes; Saartjie's image might be tailored to fulfill European fantasies about "Hottentots." The three men conspired to take Saartjie to England and option the rights to her exhibition on a contract basis. They also planned to ship to London a giraffe skin, still a rarity in Britain. Inspired by the brisk trade in the ethnographically unusual fueled by scientific imperialism, Dunlop and Cesars persuaded themselves that a pretty maidservant with notable buttocks and a spotty giraffe skin were a winning combination on which to stake their future.

As a military surgeon trained in Britain, Dunlop was well aware of the exploitative potential of live human exhibits. London had a thriving entertainment trade in human and scientific curiosities, and a person from an almost mythical African race might provide an exceptional draw for novelty-hungry British audiences. Hunter and tradesman Pieter Cesars was familiar with foreign explorers and botanists who paid good money for all manner of collectibles to ship back to Europe. Styling themselves men of science, many eighteenth-century ethnobotanical tourists and collectors such as Sir Joseph Banks called at the Cape Colony; others, like Carl Linnaeus, paid high prices from afar for its exotica.

The first impediment to the plan to take Saartjie to England was that it was illegal. Under the Hottentot Proclamation implemented the previous year, no Khoisan person was permitted to leave the colony without the direct permission of the governor. The second problem was that Saartjie might prove intractable. She would need careful persuasion. It can only be imagined how Dunlop and the Cesars brothers presented this plan to Saartjie, and what promises, inducements, and threats they made.

At the beginning of February 1810 Dunlop applied to the government requesting permission to take his male slave (unnamed in official documentation) with him to England as a servant-apprentice. Lord Caledon's secretary Henry Alexander authorized the request, providing that "proper precautions are taken to secure the freedom of the Boy hereafter." Dunlop then applied to the collector of customs Charles Blair, from whom he was also required to request an apprenticeship for this slave so that he could gain permission to travel. Blair, however, was away, not due to return until the end of March.

On March 16 Dunlop wrote to the governor's office and explained impatiently that "being obliged to embark Monday next," he could wait no longer for certification from the collector's office. Pressured by Dunlop, Blair's deputy Thomas Ord confirmed in writing that before his departure Blair had given his verbal approval, "provided it meet the Governor's approbation." "Mr. Ord," Dunlop assured the governor's office, pressing his advantage, "will take care to get you a written certificate from Mr Blair the moment he returns."

Because Hendrik Cesars was not a white man, he too required permission to leave the Cape Colony. On March 7, Hendrik went to the governor's office armed with this intriguing letter from his master:

The bearer Hendrik Cezar, wishes to take the opportunity of going to England under my protection, and will be greatly obliged, if you will alter his pass or grant him a new one, which ever you think proper. He would have availed himself of going along with a friend of his, who went in the *Wilhelmina* but was prevented by sickness.

The *Wilhelmina* was a British coasting schooner captained by Daniel Tack that plied cargoes of salt between Saldanha Bay on the west coast and Cape Town. She had sailed from Table Bay on March 4, three days before Cesars went to Lord Caledon's office to request permission to travel. The identity of Cesars's "friend" is unknown, which makes Dunlop's letter ambiguous.

Piecing together the fragments of evidence of the plan to smuggle Saartjie to England, it seems that she sailed the short local passage from Cape Town to Saldanha Bay on the *Wilhelmina* on March 4, escorted by trusted accomplice Pieter Cesars. She was lifted aboard ship by merchant seamen given the nod, and perhaps an extra ration of brandy for their connivance, by Captain Tack.

As an officer and military surgeon, Dunlop and his entourage would take passage on a navy ship, documented and cleared for departure at busy Table Bay, where passenger lists were officially logged. The Hottentot Proclamation made it impossible for Saartjie to travel legally with Dunlop from Cape Town without the authorization of the governor. However, as every illegal slaver knew, merchant seamen were easier to bribe than military captains. Saldanha Bay was garrisoned, but remote. Navy transport ships took on cargo at Saldanha, making it feasible to smuggle Saartjie aboard during the hectic bustle of winching and stowage. Additional travelers taken aboard at Saldanha should, of course, have been added to the ship's log, but for the right price it was always possible to slip a stowaway aboard.

On March 20 Dunlop received permission from the Governor's office to depart from the Cape, "together with his servant, on board the *Diadem Transport* commanded by William Davison [Master], bound to England." Approved by Lord Caledon, Dunlop's permission for departure was signed by Henry Alexander.

Two days before Cesars set sail for England, Anna Catharina and he visited the public notary's office to amend their will, making their adopted daughter their universal heir.

The *Diadem* set sail from Cape Town on April 1, 1810, captained by William Davison, with an English crew of twenty-two sailors and five boys. A five-hundred-ton, sixty-four-gun troop ship, *Diadem* was on her way back for refitting at Chatham dockyard, where she had been built in 1782.

The baggage brought by Dunlop and Cesars included the huge, smelly giraffe skin, wrapped and rolled like a fermenting Turkish carpet in the cargo hold. The transport of the skin of a camelopardalis, or what Shelley called "the spotted camelopard," was still so unusual as to be newsworthy, and Dunlop's precious, bulky cargo attracted interest as it was loaded aboard ship. This noisy, highly visible event was in stark contrast to the silent, muffled embarkation of a young woman when the *Diadem* called in at Saldanha Bay.

Saartjie had no official permission to travel to England. By government decree, her papers would have had to be presented to the master, and her name entered in the log, but the ship's musters for the *Diadem* from December 14, 1809, to June 20, 1810, are missing from Admiralty records. It was wartime, and HMS *Diadem,* temporarily decommissioned pending her refurbishment, did not travel empty back to England. No doubt the *Diadem* would have taken cargo on board at Saldanha Bay such as grain or salt, and, amid the bustle, a female stowaway.

Saartjie's roguish managers succeeded in spiriting her out of the Cape Colony. Orphaned and unprotected, bereft of a mother's counsel, or of older women to offer cautionary tales, Saartjie was vulnerable to coercion and the promises made to her by Dunlop and Cesars. Economically dependent, she was not in a position to negotiate. With hindsight it is easy to see that Saartjie was lured across the world to her doom. However, the promise of new adventure offered some palliative solace for her losses, trauma, and miseries. What was left to keep Saartjie in Cape Town? It is not hard to see how she was persuaded to exchange interminable domestic servitude for the enticements of a regular wage, the possibility of greater freedom in England, and even the hope of fame and fortune. In a crucial piece of evidence, Saartjie later said that Dunlop had "promised to send her back rich." It is clear that Saartjie expected to return home. Dunlop and Cesars guaranteed to send her back to Cape Town after a period of six years in England, with "the money belonging to her," and at their expense.

As the *Wilhelmina* sailed away from Cape Town it is unlikely Saartjie looked on Table Mountain with any wistfulness. She was not free, but she was freer than many. Any freedom was better than none.

By means of a short voyage on the *Wilhelmina* from Cape Town to Saldanha Bay, from where the *Diadem* carried her off to England,

Saartjie was smuggled from South Africa. Her understandable trepi-
dation at embarking clandestinely, and with an all-male crew, might
have been mingled with a sense of naïve expectation. She was young,
resilient, and seemed adventurous. She knew she was not traveling
afar to remain just a domestic servant; no one got rich from that. Was
she looking forward to being wealthy, as Dunlop and Cesars had
promised? Was she curious about what it meant to be starting a new
life as a representative of her people, or utterly mystified by the
whole proposition?

The Cape Peninsula is best surveyed from the lofty top of the
Adamastor-like Table Mountain. On a sun-drenched, cloudless day,
the arc of the horizon is seemingly illimitable, as if the eye were
falling off the edge of the world, and the elated, uncertain heart im-
pelled to follow its leap. Sky and ocean shift through the spectrum of
colors of hope and yearning, from dazzling cerulean blue, to violet,
indigo, and softly muted silver-gray.

Viewed from the vantage point of the mountain, the ship would
have looked like a toy. Yet for earthbound Saartjie, sailing beneath
the waterline beyond her farthest horizons must have been an experience filled with mystery, physical discomfort, and fear. In this great
wide expanse of seascape, Saartjie's world contracted to wind and
sails, permanently damp and salty clothes, bitter food, a tiny scrap of
sleeping space beneath a hammock—and no clear picture of what
lay ahead.

Chapter 5
VENUS RISING

HE VENUS OF ANCIENT MYTHOLOGY, goddess of love and desire, rose naked from the foaming sea and stepped ashore onto a small island where grass and flowers sprang from the soil wherever she trod. The Seasons hastened to clothe and adorn her. Saartjie, however, arrived in England an illicit, precariously positioned immigrant. HMS *Diadem* made landfall in Plymouth in May 1810. Saartjie stepped ashore wearing sea-damp servant's smocking and inadequate rawhide shoes. Her few personal possessions included her sheepskin kaross, musical instruments, and tortoiseshell pendant.

While Saartjie may have been wishing for dry, warm clothes and stronger shoes, Dunlop and Cesars made arrangements to transport the giraffe skin and a trunk containing the accessories with which they would array Saartjie as a Hottentot Venus. This collection included ivory bracelets, ostrich-shell necklaces, wood and bone bead belts, anklets, earrings, an elaborate headband, and an imposing and intricately wrought bridal necklace. There were also ostrich feathers, an assortment of pipes, and a bushbuck apron of the design worn by rural women to cover their genitals, for modesty.

Huddled together on unsteady land legs awaiting the first stagecoach to London, the bluff military surgeon and his sea-dazed companions must have resembled nothing so much as a traveling showman with his troupe of curiosities hung about by musical instruments, sea chests, and the outsized giraffe skin.

As Saartjie entered the mighty wilderness of London, perhaps her senses were overwhelmed by the whirl and uproar of its tumultuous streets, smelling of dung and smoke. Insignificant and anonymous as she entered its vortex, Saartjie could little imagine that within two months she would be singled out as the talk of Europe's biggest metropolis.

Dunlop, still on full officer's pay, took lodgings for the entourage on York Street, off St. James's Square, and hired an additional black manservant. York Street was in the center of the golden square mile where the idle rich danced, gambled, gossiped, and shopped their way through the final year of the reign of George III.

A short distance away at Westminster, Parliament debated the success of Wellington's campaign to hold Portugal against the French.

St. James's Palace was larger than any building Saartjie had ever seen, and Whitehall still startlingly white. She was among the first people to experience the artificial illumination of central London; the city's newfangled experiment with gas streetlights provided "a vivid white . . . brilliant light," and gave the streets of Piccadilly by night the luminosity of a dream.

Saartjie heard the unfamiliar, flat-vowelled voices of Londoners. She saw African and Indian men in European suits; white women in brightly colored and precariously balanced silk turbans, ostrich plumes, and Indian shawls; children of all races in rags; and tripe stalls festooned with slick entrails, penny a cup.

St. James's Square had been London's most fashionable district since the Restoration. Saartjie had illustrious neighbors in Piccadilly, many of whom she was to meet, including not only Beau Brummell but Tom Sheridan and his father, the playwright Richard Brinsley Sheridan, member of Parliament for Ilchester. Lord Grenville, whose name would be publicly linked with Saartjie's, lived nearby in Cleveland Square. Grenville was a leading campaigner against slavery; he worked alongside Charles James Fox, leader of the liberal Whig party, and carried the resolutions in favor of abolition in June 1806. Piccadilly's reputation as a magnet for artists had been established in the eighteenth century; John Gay, William Hogarth, Alexander Pope, Jonathan Swift, and George Frideric Handel all immortalized it in their works, and enjoyed the hospitality of their patrons in its grand houses.

Late Georgian Piccadilly was also the epicenter of science and showmanship. Sir Joseph Banks presided over London's Royal Society at Somerset House nearby, in the Strand. Banks became famous as the botanist on Captain Cook's first voyage to Australia in 1768. Enlightenment scientists, medics, doctors, naturalists, and explorers saw themselves as quite distinct from the showmen, crackpots, and quacks who plied their entertainments day after day about Piccadilly; but in the public mind they were generally regarded as one and the same. Banks strove to convince the government that serious scientific research was an economic and political necessity for imperial expansion, but his nickname, the Botanic Macaroni, illustrates the irreverence with which he was popularly regarded.

Many of the specimens Banks collected on Cook's South Seas expedition were displayed in Bullock's Liverpool Museum at 22 Piccadilly, described at the beginning of 1810 by *Bell's Weekly Messenger* as "the most fashionable place of amusement in London." The Liverpool Museum was the creation of traveler and naturalist William Bullock, a close friend of Banks, who had purchased many curiosities from Cook's voyages.

In August, while Saartjie was still adjusting to English beer and mutton pies, Dunlop approached London's most successful museum master with a commercial proposition. Dunlop offered to sell Bullock his "camel-opard skin of great beauty and considerable value," brought recently from the Cape of Good Hope. Dunlop also revealed that he was, as Bullock put it, "in possession of a Hottentot Woman," who was available to be contracted for exhibition for two years. After this period, Dunlop explained, he "was under an engagement to return her to the Cape of Good Hope." Dunlop emphasized "the extraordinary shape and make of the woman," stressing her value as "an object of great curiosity" and arguing that she "would make the fortune of any person by exhibiting her (for the said two years) to the public." Suspiciously, this two-year period contradicted Saartjie's later claim that her contractual period was six years.

Liverpudlian Bullock had already made his fortune. Starting as a jeweler-silversmith, he began to collect rare specimens of natural history from the captains and crews of returning ships, chiefly James Cook. Bullock opened his first exhibition of diverse natural and artificial curiosities in Liverpool in 1795. In 1809 he moved Bullock's Liverpool Museum to London, where, within a month of opening, it became the city's most successful attraction. By June the following year, eighty thousand people had entered the doors, and a permanent queue stretched outside.

Bullock's catalogue boasted that his exhibition included "upwards of 7000 Natural and Foreign Curiosities, antiquities, and productions of the fine arts." He was the first English museum director to organize his specimens according to their habitat groups, and to display his objects with a choreographer's care for posture and appropriate environment. Bullock admired Dunlop's giraffe skin, beautifully spotted with dark brown on a cream-colored ground. Once stuffed, it would be nearly twice the height of a full-grown elephant and would provide a newsworthy addition to his famous Artificial Forest, the centerpiece of his museum. After two meetings, the men agreed to terms on the skin. However, Bullock flatly rejected Dunlop's distasteful proposal to sell him the right to exhibit the "Hottentot Woman," declaring that "such an exhibition would not meet the countenance of the public." He was a museum director, not the keeper of a freak show.

Bullock did not, as yet, exhibit live human curiosities. A member of a host of learned societies, including the Horticultural, Geological, and Wernerian societies, the well-connected Bullock regarded himself as a respectable businessman. Significantly, at the time Dunlop offered him Saartjie's contract, Bullock was trying to get himself elected as a fellow of the Linnean Society. Although he eventually succeeded, Bullock's proposal as a candidate caused protest among some of the society's members, who blackballed him as a quack "who by the puffs with which he daily fills the newspapers is likely to bring that hitherto respectable body into disrepute." Bullock also moved in abolitionist circles, and was wary of the possibility that Saartjie, a member of a subject nation, might have been brought to England against her will. Bullock felt a genuine ethical objection to Dunlop's proposal, but it was also the case that involvement in Saartjie's exhibition might scupper his entry to the Linnean Society, and dent his cultivated propriety.

Master and servant's dreams of quick riches foundered, but, notably, Dunlop did not seek to solve the problem by selling Saartjie's performance rights to one of London's many established freak-show impresarios. With no reputable alternative exhibitors to approach, Dunlop and Cesars determined to manage Saartjie's exhibition themselves.

Saartjie needed to do more than just shift, pout, and wiggle around the stage to entice jaded London audiences to part with the two-shilling ticket price. Here, Saartjie's musical skills and exhilarating, misspent evenings in the Cape taverns came into play. Saartjie had brought with her from Cape Town her *ramkie* and a bowed lute. Dunlop and Cesars importuned her to perform her repertoire of folk songs in Afrikaans and Khoi. She would also be required to dance a little, "in the manner of her country." The Hottentot Venus exhibition would open for four hours, six days a week, placing a heavy demand on Saartjie, who would need the ingenuity to devise an engaging routine and the stamina to repeat it throughout the long afternoon shows.

Location was critical. Dunlop and Cesars reasoned correctly that a venue near the Liverpool Museum might pick up business from the crowds pressing to see Bullock's novelties. They secured 225 Piccadilly, on the north side of the thoroughfare, diagonally across the street from the Liverpool Museum.

Piccadilly was the heart of London's brisk trade in natural and artificial human freaks, curiosities, "wonders," and popular entertainments. A *Punch* cartoon entitled "Deformito-mania" captures the district's nature as the center of the amusement trade, with its exhibitionist excess of exaggeration and theatrical expostulation.

The cartoon shows riotous hordes of well-heeled, top-hatted men and fashionably dressed, bonneted women crowding through the doors of the Hall of Wonder, whose street front is plastered with sensationalist signs. THIS IS THE NE PLUS ULTRA OF HIDEOUSNESS, ACKNOWLEDGED SUCH BY THE PRESS! is pasted next to the Hall of Ugliness, which in turn promises THE GREATEST DEFORMITY IN THE WORLD WITHIN: NO CONNECTION WITH DEFORMITY NEXT DOOR; and, next door, BY FAR THE UGLIEST BIPED IS HERE, ONE SHILLING.

The entertainment trade in human deformities specialized in live exhibits. Many acts were straightforward exploitations of human variation and disease for which there was not as yet any medical remedy. Siamese twins and albino children (advertised as "White Negroes") were paraded at street fairs throughout the eighteenth century. In June 1810, a West Indian child advertised as "the Piebald Boy" was put on show in the Strand. Those who suspected he was painted were invited to scratch or rub him on the promise that they would soon find out he was genuinely mottled. Other popular freak shows in the area included "the Fasting Woman of Tetbury"; fifty-stone Daniel Lambert, or Fat Dan, the fattest man who ever lived; Frenchman Claude Ambroise Seurat, "the Living Skeleton," conversely the thinnest; and nineteen-and-a-half-inch Caroline Crachami, the miniature "Sicilian Fairy."

The concept of a Hottentot Venus fitted well with the Piccadilly tradition of goddesses, sea marvels, and other mythical creatures that had been attached to the area from its earliest days. The famous Water-Theatre of the ingenious Mr. Winstanley (boxes two shillings) offered sea gods and goddesses, nymphs, mermaids, satyrs, and later even flying dragons. At 225 Piccadilly, Saartjie would therefore be exhibiting in the acknowledged home of theatrical curiosities from beneath and across the ocean.

Inspired by Bullock's carefully orchestrated settings for his exhibits, Dunlop and Cesars got to work on setting the stage at 225 Piccadilly in a manner that would invoke a sense of Africa. They commissioned the painting of wooden flats depicting the pastoral landscape and flora of Africa. These framed the centerpiece of the set, a grass hut signifying Saartjie's home. For the exhibition of a human curiosity at the beginning of the nineteenth century, it was a lot of scenery.

Saartjie's Venus costume was vital to the success of the show. Above all, it was necessary to create the illusion of Saartjie's semi-nakedness onstage. Her ensemble, though not strictly typical of a Khoisan woman, "was at any rate suggestive of South Africa." Londoners had long been familiar with rumors about the extraordinary shape of Hottentot women, but the opportunity to see such a woman in the flesh was a novelty.

Dunlop and Cesars wanted to demonstrate that Saartjie's bottom, the source of her potential fame, was a bona fide physiological anomaly, and to hint at the legendary extended labia attributed to Khoisan women. The accessories brought from Cape Town provided the adornment for Saartjie's Venus costume; they were arranged over her "fleshings," a tailor-made one-piece body stocking, or leotard, fashioned from a figure-hugging fabric of silk and cotton. Saartjie was measured and fitted for this bespoke silken garment, designed to make her appear as nature made her. To be realistic, it needed to fit as snugly as a second skin. Fostering the fallacy of Saartjie's bared flesh, all the publicity images concealed the seams, buttons, and hooks that held the fleshings tightly in place, making it cling to every contour of her body. To conceal where this garment ended at her neck, hands, and ankles, Saartjie arranged abundant jewelry and adornments. A torrent of ostrich-shell and bead necklaces cascaded in shiny strings from her décolletage. Jangling cuffs of bracelets, possibly ivory, hung from each of her wrists, and ostrich-feather anklets studded with beads brushed her slippered feet.

Hung about with necklaces, belts, and ostrich plumes, Saartjie's outer garment was a skimpy mesh of beads and feathers. A rectangular apron embroidered and edged with pearly beading was placed strategically above her pubic bone, her Mound of Venus. From underneath this pubic camouflage hung vertically descending pendants of hide cured to a malleable texture of buttery softness, each tapering into a rippling striped cord, finished with ostrich-feather tassels, like a row of silken bell-pulls, brushing the bows on Saartjie's slippers. It was an elaborate, exaggerated female codpiece of dramatic size. The effect of its soft folds, fur fringes, and pendulous extensions was to imply that its purpose was to modestly conceal the supposed elongated labia of a Hottentot woman, made legendary by the uncorroborated claims of numerous European travelers to the Cape.

The complexity of the apparel meant Saartjie needed help dressing. She said that she had "two Black Boys to wait upon her" at York Street, and explained that either Dunlop or Cesars "assists her in the morning when she is nearly completely attired, for the purposes of fastening the Ribbon around her waist." Saartjie used greasepaint, kohl, powder, combs, and oil to make up her face and hair.

There is no written record of the origin of Saartjie's Venus sobriquet. It was a classical reference; but more than that, Venus was simply a synonym for sex. In the same period, "Hottentot" signified all that was other: strange, disturbing, culturally alien, sexually deviant, and excessive. United, the words "Hottentot" and "Venus" carried a potent force. They coupled Eros with notions of ugliness, desire with degradation, license with taboo, transcendent goddess with carnal beast; they articulated the alarming siren allure of feminine concupiscence, Aristotle's fascinating, terrifying *animal avidum generandi*— "the beast greedy for generation." These highfalutin Latin tags were not, however, the slang the ballad criers used to advertise Saartjie's putatively extraordinary pudenda to passersby.

On Wednesday September 12, Sir Joseph Banks at the Royal Society received his invitation to attend Saartjie's exclusive preview on the following Monday, as did other members of London's social elite and intelligentsia. On Thursday September 20, the famous advertisements announcing the opening of the Hottentot Venus exhibition to the public appeared in the *Morning Herald* and the *Morning Post*. Written by Dunlop, these advertisements took care to cast Cesars—"a native of the Cape"—in the role of Saartjie's *foreign* manager.

Saartjie first performed in front of a paying public audience at lunchtime on Monday September 24. What went through her mind, what emotions and physical sensations did she experience that day in her very first show, stepping out onto the elevated platform, exposed in her new, unfamiliar costume? Uncertainty, bemusement, anxiety, the adrenaline rush of fear? For the first time, Saartjie was raised at head height above those around her, an entirely new perspective.

The exhibition room glowed with torches, candles, and oil lamps, illuminating the small stage at one end, with its centerpiece grass hut and painted flats of the "African interior," all up-lit by reflectors contrived from mirrors and colored water. At the back of the stage was a curtained recess, where Saartjie waited as the room filled with customers, shuffling with curiosity and expectation.

Like other human curiosities, freak acts, and floor shows, the Hottentot Venus exhibition was a choreographed routine. It opened with Saartjie emerging from the hut, at the summons of Cesars. Saartjie took up a downstage position, struck up a folk song on her *ramkie,* and began to sing and dance. Observers remarked that she had "a fairly good ear" and sang pleasingly well, but that playing and dancing were her stronger talents. She strummed, she hummed, she strutted and wriggled and sashayed and sang. She sang folk and popular songs in Khoi, Afrikaans, and English, some to tunes easily recognizable to her London audience, although Dunlop and Cesars preferred her to sing traditional folk songs, in order to emphasize her strangeness and African authenticity.

Of all the sounds that defined Saartjie, her *ramkie* was the most distinguishing. In the evolution of this African guitar is compréssed the diversity of six hundred years of South African history. Descended from the original Khoi gourd and nut instruments, the *ramkie* merged, through trade routes, colonization, and slavery, with influences from Portugal and the east (mainly India and Malaysia) and later developed into the tin-can guitar. By the early nineteenth century its arpeggios carried African, Asian, Arab, and Western harmonies; this music was a direct antecedent to the blues.

Physicality has its own language: rhythms, secret chords, minor falls and major lifts. As instantly became evident from sensational responses to her performance, Saartjie was a subtle and imposing artist of the bodily form. Press descriptions of her performance offered transient, elusive glimpses of her personality: wry humor, anger, sensual self-composure, deft movement, refusal, stoicism, confrontation, all were part of Saartjie's arsenal of engagement.

Almost overnight, London was taken with Saartjie-mania. She instantly captured the public imagination. After centuries of myths and traveler's tall tales, London finally had a real, live, singing and dancing Hottentot Venus who appeared to confirm the fabulous myths and legends peddled for centuries about extraordinarily formed Hottentot women. Saartjie became London's most popular novelty. In the course of just one week she went from anonymous, recently arrived illegal immigrant to one of the city's most talked-about women, her image ubiquitous, her name swapped with wide-eyed murmurs between gossiping socialites, and bawled by newsboys on the streets.

There was an outpouring of "Sartjee"-themed popular poesy, ballads, broadsheet caricatures, articles, and printed satires. Her image proliferated, seemingly everywhere reproduced, on brightly colored posters pasted in shop windows, on penny prints held aloft by street sellers, the human tabloids who raised the cry of "Sartjee" and "Hottentot" throughout the metropolis.

Every day except Sundays, Saartjie also gave exclusive private evening views, restricted to parties of twelve, which had to be booked twenty-four hours beforehand. Night and day, Saartjie was the subject, object, be-all, and obsessively ogled-at end-all of the show. The success of the Hottentot Venus depended upon a contradiction: Saartjie needed to be perceived as a unique novelty, while absolutely typifying the stereotype of a Hottentot. Africans in England were no longer of themselves a remarkable curiosity. The permanent black population of Britain at the beginning of the nineteenth century was about twenty thousand, with numbers steadily rising following abolition in 1807. London was already multiethnic.

To promote her novelty, Saartjie's managers focused on accentuating her difference. They aimed to persuade audiences that the Hottentot Venus had a bottom unequaled by any to be seen in Lon-

don. A verse published in the *Morning Herald* demonstrates how the
London media responded:

> *Though Venus, of old,*
> *By records, we're told,*
> *Excited the praise of mankind;*
> *Our Hottentot, still,*
> *Let her die when she will,*
> *Will not leave her equal* behind.

Bottoms were big in Georgian England. From low to high culture of
all forms, Britain was a nation obsessed by buttocks, bums, arses, posteriors, derrières, and every possible metaphor, joke, or pun that
could be squeezed from this fundamental cultural obsession. From
the front parlor to Parliament, to prostitution and pornography,
Georgian England both exuberantly celebrated and earnestly de-
plored excess, grossness, and the uncontainable. Much of Saartjie's
success was a result of a simple phenomenon: with her shimmying,
voluptuous bottom, she perfectly captured the zeitgeist of late-
Georgian Britain.

Handbills and poster advertisements promoted Saartjie as a natural wonder, a new and wonderful "specimen" of a little-known tribe,
whose buttocks and suggestively fringed labial Venus apron shaped
her mystery. To some degree this was marketing hokum, as Khoisan
people had been visiting London, and attracting considerable public
attention, since the seventeenth century. None of them, however,
had been suggestively clad, generously endowed proto-showgirls.
The exaggerated claims made about Saartjie's "tribal" history were
an accepted convention of Piccadilly showmanship. Whatever Dunlop's pretensions to provide scientific and cultural illumination to
the literati, Saartjie was a sexpot Venus, who showed her legs. The
use of the Venus sobriquet was a clever marketing technique, offering audiences the enticement to see a naked African goddess. But
Saartjie must have wondered what the audiences really came to see.

Saartjie became the most famous theatrical attraction in Piccadilly in the transition between two distinct historical moments in English racial attitudes. She arrived toward the end of the era when sentimental primitivism held sway, and at the beginning of the rise of the new pseudoscience of ethnology, in which human beings became living specimens. Ethnology went hand in white cotton glove and khaki pith-helmet with imperialism, the economic exploitation of Africa, and the emergence of scientific racism. Saartjie's time in London coincided with a new era of European imperialist expansion into the African interior, feminized by its would-be British colonizers as a continent ripe for conquest. Dovetailing with this was the fact that African otherness, with its implications of the alien and strange, had an appeal long exploited by theatrical and popular entertainments. The Hottentot Venus arose in London as the very apotheosis of Europe's invented Africa, the dark continent of feminized impenetrability and crude potency.

VERY SOON, the metropolitan elite began to summon Saartjie to their grand houses to entertain dinner and party guests. One of her most memorable private audiences was with the ultimate Regency rake, William, the fourth Duke of Queensbury; known as Old Q, he was famed as a millionaire, an amateur jockey, and a debauched voluptuary. Queensbury expired in bed on December 23, 1810, at the age of eighty-six, surrounded by seventy love letters from as many women, crying "Billet-doux!" with his dying breath.

A month before he died, Old Q invited Saartjie to a dinner party at his lavish mansion at 138 and 139 Piccadilly, where he was said to bathe daily in a silver bath filled with milk. Queensbury was the last of the nobility to keep running footmen, one of whom was sent to 225 Piccadilly to instruct the management that the Hottentot Venus was required for an audience with the duke, who sent a sedan chair to collect her. The *Morning Herald* reported:

A few evenings since, the *Hottentot Venus* paid a chair visit to a venerable Duke, who still preserves a taste for CHOICE things. After a microscopic inspection of her prominent beauties, she

danced . . . to the exquisite satisfaction of his Grace, and a select party of *Amateurs* of natural productions.

The press revealed that Saartjie "danced an African fandango in a
style of true savage simplicity" and then bathed in Old Q's silver tub,
her bottom described as "the tempting crust of a well rasped roll
floating in a tureen of savoury soup." Lord Grenville, Sir Joseph
Banks, and the poet R. P. Knight attended, prompting *The Satirist* to
a spoof. Queensbury, the parody proposed, formed a committee to
ascertain whether or not the Hottentot Venus had, as rumored, an
ancestral connection to the house of Buckingham, and could therefore be claimed as a direct relative of the big-bottomed Lord
Grenville. Given his political position, Lord Grenville's broad flanks
were a gift to the press.

It was evident that George III would soon leave the throne. Pun-
dits believed that when the Prince Regent succeeded his father, he
would dissolve Parliament and invite Lord Grenville and his Whig
coalition to take over. To all of England, Lord Grenville and his fol-
lowers had been known as the broad bottoms since the short-lived
Grenville-Fox coalition of 1806, the so-called Ministry of all the Talents. Saartjie's rise to fame in England was coincident with the time
when politics and press were preoccupied with the fate of the broad
bottomites, who, it was believed, would soon be running Parliament
once again. The convergence of Lord Grenville's broad bottom with
Saartjie's was a journalist's dream. The ceaseless outpouring of prose
caricature and cartoons owes much to this coincidence. The obsession with Saartjie's posterior, posterity, and broad bottomedness and
the endless punning on rear ends, rumps, fundaments, and fat arses
became explicitly tied to the most pressing and topical political issues concerning the decline of King George, the rise of the Regency,
and which rumps would take over government. Rumps also had dan-
gerously republican connotations from the Rump Parliament of
1649–1653.

In this context, Saartjie's visit to Queensbury, a close friend of
Lord Grenville, set the scene for fulsome satire. *The Satirist* immortal-

ized the encounter with an imagined scene. When they entered his
parlor, Old Q informed his illustrious guests that Saartjie was about
to have a milk bath in his famous tub, and that he had "offered to of-
ficiate at the ablutionary rites." In the narrator's voyeuristic fantasy,
Saartjie slips into the tub in a posture of submission, to the duke's delight.

> So floated the distinguishing feature of the interesting Hot-
> tentot in the lacteal bath, the rest of her body being com-
> pletely immersed, so gazed, with anxious eye his grace of
> Queensbury. Having tired her fine form with studious and
> tender care, he informed his valet that the milkman might
> now have the milk for his customers, and handed her to the
> parlour.

Sir Joseph Banks then took Saartjie's measurements with his "newly
invented instrument called a '*gloutometer*', with which, he claimed, he
would quickly discover if there were any affinity between the
Grenville and the Hottentot protuberances." Queensbury, hovering
lecherously, suggested that a more reliable comparison might be
made by inviting some of Lord Grenville's big-bottomed female relations for inspection. Sir Joseph Banks's ethnographic bottom-
measuring experiment concluded, Queensbury insisted that Saartjie
remain "beneath his hospitable roof till next morning. She politely
acceded to his request, and, of course, felt highly gratified by his
grace's kind attentions."

Speculations on Saartjie's impressions of London became a particularly favored subject for satire. Journalists took the opportunity
to poke fun at native English culture through the eyes of this new
South African naïf. Far off the geographical mark, satires always rendered Saartjie's voice in mock Anglo-Jamaican patois.

"De Hottentot Fenus" commented, with sparkling wit and tren-
chant observation, on newsworthy matters whose relevance has long
since past, such as the dispute over the rising cost of bread due to the
war with Napoleon's empire. Sometimes couched within these topi-

calities were scenes that gained their humorous force by playing on Saartjie's reputation for forthright behavior and quick temper. The *Morning Post,* for instance, ran a spoof letter from "De Hottentot Fenus To De Gret Lord Grinwell, who desire her to write him what she tink of dis country." She is visited by a politician "from debate shop" who "den introduce beauty from Forum," but Venus is unimpressed.

> I laugh at her, she so dam frightful. He den say he want me speak with her, at debate shop; I say me no go where such a set. Den he grin, *Beauty* frown, me no care. Debate man repeat nonsense, he want me speak; I laugh louder—he fool, may go Newgate. I turn *back* on him, and *send him out of room.* Beauty faint; dat very common, she used to it. I give slap of face; she come back, get up, and say, "I rise blow you up, you damn *Hot*tentot." I give her another slap; she ran out, and called Jack. Her leave an old wig behind, and little beggarly bag; cosmetics in it and little cards—dem me told tickets of *pawn man.* Dat very bad; oh fie! she sad one.

For publicity, Dunlop and Cesars arranged for Saartjie to take regular Sunday carriage rides around central London. From her carriage Saartjie could see the lime trees in St. James's Park, their summer foliage bottle green under a pale, diffuse, sheepskin sky. Those who saw Venus's coach pass—street sellers, rag-and-bone men, the rushing or loitering London crowds—pressed to catch a look at the now-famous African icon. From amid the cacophony, Saartjie would have heard her Anglicized name, "Sartjee," belted out in the sensational verses of the ballad criers. On shopfronts, street corners, and newspaper stalls she could see posters bearing the image of her stage self, reflected back at her, vivid with aquatint, larger than life. Was that really supposed to be her, that woman standing in exaggerated profile, breasts and buttocks aloft, dressed like a tribal bride, looking determinedly ahead, pipe in her mouth, smoke curling upwards?

Chapter 6

FREEWOMAN, OR SLAVE?

A FORTNIGHT INTO HER EXHIBITION, Saartjie caught the flu. London was frenetic with talk about the Hottentot Venus; the name of "Sartjee" could be seen and heard from Seven Dials to St. Paul's. It was not a good time to be sick.

Saartjie sneezed her way through the repetitive performances with increasingly aching limbs. One afternoon, matters came to a head when a spectator challenged Cesars about her ill health. Cesars retorted that she "was always sulky when company was there," but Saartjie pointed to her throat and her knees "as if she felt pain in both, pleading with tears that he would not force her compliance." Unmoved, Cesars brandished his bamboo walking stick at Saartjie, and told her to get on with it; a witness remarked, "She saw it, knew its power, and, though ill, delayed no longer." It was a pathetic tableau, charged with the menace of a real domestic violence that many believed was replicated in the offstage relationship between showgirl and manager.

While Saartjie played her guitar, "a gentleman chanced to laugh" at her. Roused by "sickness, servitude," and fury, she "endeavoured to strike him with the musical instrument." Cesars capitalized on the drama, declaring his Venus "wild as a beast." Many of the spectators were all too willing to agree.

This episode set the pattern for many similar instances of Saartjie's publicly exhibited discontent. She protested—noisily, physically, viscerally—against the unscrupulous hucksters who exploited her, and against offensive customers. The heightened element of personal drama in the dynamic of threat and grudging submission added an intense atmosphere of kinetic, unsettling energy. The show reinforced the expected relationship between white master and black slave, and audiences little questioned its authenticity. Saartjie was perceived as a temperamentally unpredictable "native," and Cesars believed to be one of those devilish Boers so recently routed by the moral might of the British.

As a result of her forceful public displays of displeasure, Saartjie attracted the attention of antislavery campaigners. A letter to the editor of *The Examiner* on Sunday October 21, written by abolitionist Zachary Macaulay, protested:

> To a contemplative and feeling man few things are so painful as to behold the degradation of his species: under whatever disguise the spectacle may be veiled, whether as an object of science or natural research, it is nevertheless a disgusting, afflictive and mortifying sight.

"By her gestures and sighs she seemed evidently depressed, and evinced a sullen reluctance to obey the commands of her keeper," chafed *The Sporting Magazine,* likening Cesars to a slave owner, circus ringmaster, or animal tamer. In one final image of animal debasement it stated that Saartjie was "shewn like a chained beast." This simile, used to gain public sympathy, created the myth that Saartjie performed to the public chained, and in a cage. Although many women have appeared both before and since on leashes, chained, or in cages, both literally enslaved and enslaved for popular entertainment, Saartjie was not one of them.

Saartjie was caught in the contradictions of Enlightenment redefinitions of human freedom. In legal terms, abolition made the difference between slavery and servitude a question of self-possession, not escape from economic poverty. But for Saartjie, there were also economic advantages to be gained.

"No nation in Europe . . . has . . . plunged so deeply into this guilt as Great Britain," said William Pitt the Younger of the slave trade in

1792. In 1803 Henry Brougham reminded Parliament that "we have been the chief trader, I mean the ringleaders in the crime." Abolitionism in England, which had its roots in republican revolutionary politics, was by the early nineteenth century entangled with Christian notions of responsibility, exculpation from guilt, the quest for redemption, and free-market capitalist philanthropy.

Lord Grenville opposed slavery from the first debate in the House of Commons on the trade in 1789, the year of Saartjie's birth. Succeeding Pitt, Prime Minister Grenville, with Foreign Secretary Charles James Fox, in June 1806 moved resolutions for abolition in both houses. Lord Chancellor Thomas Erskine changed his mind in favor of abolition, and, fifteen years after William Wilberforce introduced the first abolitionist motion into Parliament, the bill passed both houses.

The liberal Duke of Gloucester became the first president of the African Institution in July 1807. Evolving from the Sierra Leone Company, the Institution's objective was "the civilization and improvement of Africa" and "the entire and universal Abolition of the Slave Trade." Its founding members included Zachary Macaulay, Lord Ellenborough, the younger William Pitt, Granville Sharp, and the Nonconformist brewer Samuel Whitbread.

The African Institution aimed to "prepare and fortify the minds of the ignorant natives of Africa against the fraudulent and mischievous efforts of eager and adventurous traffic," and to offer "some compensation for the indescribable miseries which . . . Englishmen have inflicted upon the African race." Abroad, the Institution tried to persuade African traders to exchange the slave trade for alternative business ventures that it supplied. Back home, it kept an eye out for abuses against abolition.

On Thursday October 11, Zachary Macaulay wrote a letter to the *Morning Chronicle,* the leading Whig daily newspaper. Born in 1768, son of a Scottish priest, Macaulay devoted his life to the abolition of the "abominable traffic," awakened to slavery's horrors by his youthful experiences on a sugar estate in Jamaica. He went to the island at age sixteen as a bookkeeper, was promoted to estate manager, and then resigned in disgust. He once traveled as a passenger on an English slave ship bound for the West Indies, in order to witness the horrors of the Middle Passage. In 1793 Macaulay became governor of the new colony of liberated slaves, Sierra Leone, appointed by William Wilberforce.

Macaulay had been secretary of the African Institution since it was founded in 1807. From his study overlooking Clapham High Street, Macaulay penned the opening salvo in the battle to plead the cause of "that wretched object advertised and publicly shewn for money— the Hottentot Venus." Macaulay had returned that afternoon from his first visit to 225 Piccadilly, and was morally outraged.

Macaulay described witnessing a hateful tableau of degradation and exploitation between male master and female black slave, enacted at the heart of free London. Determined to prove that Saartjie was illegally transported and enslaved, Macaulay wanted to know "under what circumstances she came to England and whether she was made a public spectacle with her own free will and consent, or whether she was compelled to exhibit herself and was desirous of returning to her own country."

During his visit, Macaulay questioned Cesars about Saartjie, and asked how she came to be in England, performing in such a manner. She is a Hottentot, explained Cesars, obtained "from the Dutch Boors" at the Cape, where "he had made an agreement with the Government and they had given him permission to take her to this Country." Macaulay declared himself "much surprised" that she was brought to England with the consent of the Cape government. Are you sure, he pressed, that the governor, Lord Caledon, gave his permission? Yes, he did, Cesars confirmed. Macaulay did not believe him, and asked if Lord Caledon's permission was in writing; Cesars insisted that indeed it was.

Unconvinced, Macaulay, who was in regular correspondence with Lord Caledon, demanded that Cesars show him the signed permission, "as he knew his hand writing." Cesars expostulated, "What won't you believe my word? I have already told you that he has signed it and shall give you no further satisfaction."

Macaulay's letter ignited a press debate over Saartjie's status as free agent or slave:

> This poor female is made to walk, to *dance,* to shew herself, not for her own advantage, but for the profit of her master, who, when she appeared tired, holds up *a stick to her, like the wild beast keepers,* to intimidate her into obedience. . . . I have read somewhere that the air of the British Constitution is too pure to permit slavery to exist where its influence extends. If that be the case, why is this poor creature to live under the most palpable and abject slavery in the very heart of the metropolis, for I am sure you will easily discriminate between those beings who are sufficiently degraded to show themselves for their *own* immediate profit, and where they act from their own free will; and this poor slave, who is obliged to shew herself, *to dance,* to be an object of the lowest ribaldry, by which her keeper is the only gainer. I am no advocate for these sights, on the contrary, I think it base in the extreme, that any human being should be thus exposed. It is contrary to every principle of morality or good order, and this exhibition connects the same offence to public decency, with that most horrid of all situations, *Slavery.*

Saartjie had an important champion in Macaulay. "Every friend to slavery knew Macaulay to be his most dangerous foe," wrote a member of the Clapham Sect. In Parliament, it was said of him, "If the Negro should be emancipated he would be more indebted to Mr Macaulay than to any other man living."

Macaulay was editor of the Evangelical *Christian Observer,* mouthpiece of the Clapham Sect, dedicated to supporting the campaign against the slave trade. Championing moral reform, the *Christian Observer* condemned theater, dancing, and novel reading. Macaulay was also an active member of the Society for the Suppression of Vice. Founded in 1802 in order to avert the moral collapse of the nation, this organization was quickly denounced for prosecuting only the poor; one commentator remarked that it should be renamed "a society for suppressing the vices of persons whose income does not exceed £500 per annum." The Society opposed "profane swearers, Sabbath-breakers, and keepers of gambling resorts and brothels," and sought "to suppress the sale of objectionable books and prints."

Macaulay held that the Hottentot Venus exhibition twinned an "offence to public decency" with the horrors of slavery. It was a formula resonant with Mary Wollstonecraft's argument, made in her *Vindication of the Rights of Women* (1792), that the sexual exploitation of women was akin to the actual condition of slavery. However, unlike Wollstonecraft, Macaulay was no supporter of women's rights. In exhorting the friends of Liberty to defend Saartjie, Macaulay called for public censure of the wanton display of her spectacular flesh, as well as an investigation into her enslaved status.

Prudery and prurience, though apparently antonyms, are common bedfellows. Wary of the feelings that her performance prompted in him, Macaulay was acutely aware of the sensual incitements of the Hottentot Venus. The abolitionists understood that Saartjie, promoted as a semiscientific ethnographic curiosity, offered sexual tourism dressed up as education. Buffed, powdered, lubricated with glistening oil, trussed in silk and cotton, adorned with feathers and beads, ethnically accessorized, face painted like a virgin sacrifice, Saartjie was got up as an embodied fetish, her costume designed to accentuate her supposed "idiosyncrasies and abnormalities." In Londoners' eyes she was the epitome of potent European fantasies about female African sexuality.

Macaulay asked his brother-in-law, the abolitionist priest Thomas Gisborne Babington, and Cape Dutch–speaking Peter Van Wageninge, to visit the exhibition and talk directly with Saartjie. Cesars confirmed that she could "speak the Dutch language," but when Van Wageninge attempted to question her, she refused to answer, presumably wary of talking in front of Cesars. She returned dejectedly to the stage, and sighed deeply throughout her "morose and sullen" performance. Babington and Van Wageninge declared that she was clearly "completely under restraint and controul and . . . deprived of her liberty."

Dunlop and Cesars hit back immediately at Macaulay's attack in a letter ghostwritten by Dunlop and published under Cesars's name. "I feel myself compelled, as a stranger," ventriloquized Dunlop, "to refute this aspersion, for the vindication of my own character, and the satisfaction of the public." The letter argued of Macaulay:

In the first point, he betrays the greatest ignorance in regard to the Hottentot, who is as free as the English. This woman was my servant at the Cape, and not my slave, much less can she be so in England, where all breathe the air of freedom; she is brought here with her own free will and consent, to be exhibited for the joint benefit of both our families. That there may be no misapprehension on the part of the public, any person who can make himself understood to her is at perfect liberty to examine her, and know from herself whether she has not been always treated, not only with humanity, but the greatest kindness and tenderness.

Dunlop was technically correct that Saartjie was Cesars's servant, and not his slave. But, as has been seen, Lord Caledon's 1809 proclamation meant that, as a Khoisan, Saartjie could not travel legitimately without the direct authorization of Lord Caledon.

Macaulay publicly demanded that Cesars produce Saartjie's passport, and "state by what ship they were brought hither; and who, if any one, besides the Captain or person with whom he engaged for their passage, are acquainted with the circumstances of their coming on board." Certain that Lord Caledon's office had never authorized Saartjie's departure, Macaulay allowed that she might have been enticed by wily persuasion, and not physical force, to embark for England:

If these circumstances be not satisfactorily cleared up, and if it should appear that a fellow-creature has been inveigled away from her home and country from motives disgraceful to human nature, all those who have been knowingly instrumental thereto, should be punished.

Cesars continued to deny that he had brought Saartjie to England "by force." He invited the public to visit 40 Haydn Square, the Minories, "where they will have an opportunity of seeing my passport from Earl Caledon, Governor of the Cape of Good Hope; and they may be further satisfied on any other point respecting my conduct."

Determined to dissuade Africans from participating in the slave trade, the African Institution was particularly critical of Cesars. Macaulay knew that Cesars was of mixed ethnicity, as was made clear in a letter to *The Examiner,* in which he compared Cesars with Shakespeare's Caliban. Despairing that the formerly oppressed becomes a future oppressor, Macaulay attacked Cesars's greed:

... what, alas! will not avarice do? It is that "stamps the monster on the man," and leads him "to play such fantastic tricks as make the angels weep".

Macaulay equally criticized Dunlop for betraying his medical calling. Rather than "a disinterested benefactor of his fellow-creatures," Dunlop had made himself a "calculating, unfeeling speculator, eager to profit from their ignorance, vice or misfortune."

Saartjie's managers tried to resolve the scandal by removing Cesars from the scene. Once again impersonating Cesars, Dunlop wrote to the press explaining that "as my mode of proceeding at the place of public exhibition seems to have given offence to the Public, I have given the sole direction of it to an Englishman, who now attends." However, this letter contradicted William Bullock, who had recently collided with Dunlop in Piccadilly. At this encounter, Bullock asked Dunlop about the Hottentot Venus exhibition. Dunlop replied that he had "been so unfortunate as to sell and dispose of his Interest in the exhibiting of the said Hottentot Woman and that he has now next to nothing to do with her."

Dunlop resented the hypocrisy of rich merchant capitalists with financial interests in African commerce dictating the morality of small-time entrepreneurs attempting their own forms of free commerce. "Pray, Mr Editor," he asked, "has she not as good a right to exhibit herself as an Irish Giant, or a Dwarf &c, &c?"

Prompted by Bullock's information, Macaulay was determined to expose Dunlop. "It is said," he wrote to the press,

> that she is, or rather was when abroad, the property of a Surgeon in the English navy, by whom her exhibitor Cezar is only employed. Sir, I do consider it necessary for the credit of our country that this affair be sifted to the end, and the real Agent be made to appear.

The balladeers quickly picked up on Macaulay's campaign. Most popular was "The storie of the Hottentot Ladie and her lawfull Knight, who essaied to release her out of captivitie, and what my lordes the judges did therein." The ballad cast Macaulay in the role of the chivalrous Sir Vikar, intent on releasing his "Hottentot Ladie." It announced Saartjie as a great rarity, living in "Piccadillie," and explained that her "rump," "large as a cauldron pot . . . is why men go to see, this lovely HOTTENTOT." The ballad continued:

> *Now this was shewn for many a day,*
> *And eke for many a night;*
> *Till sober folks began to say,*
> *That all could not be right.*
> *Some said, this was with her good will;*
> *Some said, that it was not;*
> *And asked why did they use so ill*
> *This ladie HOTTENTOT.*
>
> *At last a doughty Knight stood forth,*
> *Sir Vikar was his name;*
> *A knight of singular good worth,*

Of faire and courtly fame.
With him the laws of chivalrie
Were not so much forgot;
But he would try most gallantly,
To serve the HOTTENTOT.

The offstage dramas at the Hottentot Venus exhibition had become as diverting as the main attraction. Fought over like a disputed territory, Saartjie had no voice in the press debate over her freedom. By going to law, the African Institution aimed to give her an opportunity to have her say. Saartjie, an immigrant from a British colony, and a member of a subject people, was about to become the first black South African whose right to liberty would be put to the test of the constitutional rule of law in Britain. Saartjie was about to find herself at the center of the most contentious court case about illegal slavery since abolition.

Chapter 7
THE CASE OF THE HOTTENTOT VENUS

N Wednesday October 17, Zachary Macaulay, Thomas Gisborne Babington, and Peter Van Wageninge visited barrister Sir Simon Le Blanc at his chambers in Serjeant's Inn, Chancery Lane, to file an affidavit in support of their application for a writ of habeas corpus to be issued on Saartjie's "keepers." They demanded that Cesars be made to provide proof of Saartjie's passport from Lord Caledon, the name of the ship on which she traveled, and "whether any individuals at the 'Cape,' or elsewhere, are acquainted with the circumstances of their embarkation." Macaulay publicized the intention of the African Institution to utilize one of the fundamental tenets of the British rule of law safeguarding the liberty of the subject: "I am persuaded no English Judge would refuse a Habeas Corpus, which should assert the right of humanity."

Saartjie's abolitionist champions were determined to prove that she was compelled to exhibit herself without her free will and consent. They also wanted to know if she was "desirous of returning to her own country as the said Institution would be anxious in that case to restore her to her Country and friends." *The Examiner* opined, "Might not the Missionary Society do much by having this woman, who is very young, instructed, and then sent back to her native land?"

Macaulay's affidavit emphasized his disapproval of Saartjie's apparel: "Her dress was so tight, that her shapes above and the enormous size of her posterior parts are as visible as if the said female were naked, and the dress is evidently intended to give her the appearance of her being undressed." Macaulay then focused on the subject of Saartjie's bottom. Her "Exhibitor," he explained,

> would invite the spectators to feel her posterior parts and . . . would desire her to turn round in order that every body might see her extraordinary shape. . . . [S]he is exhibited to the public in the same manner that any animal of the brute creation would be exhibited.

Babington and Van Wageninge confirmed that members of the audience "are invited to feel her posterior parts to satisfy themselves that no art is practiced."

The abolitionists refuted Cesars's defense that Saartjie was his servant, not his slave, and therefore "as free as the English." Macaulay published an essay in *The Examiner* arguing that for a member of a subject race to be treated *like* a slave, was in effect the same as actually *being* a legal slave:

> [I]s the capture and exhibition of this Hottentot many degrees removed from the barbarous and illegal practices of the Slave Trade? . . . Let the honour of Englishmen rescue their character from the disgrace of keeping a foreigner, and a female too, in worse than Egyptian bondage.

Bullock's evidence was crucial. Bullock knew Macaulay, and both knew Sir Joseph Banks. Macaulay wrote to *The Examiner,* "[I]f it can be proved that the Hottentot has been offered to sale, this of itself would alone burst her fetters."

The case of the Hottentot Venus opened at the Court of the King's Bench in Westminster Hall, Parliament Square, on Saturday November 24, 1810. Stirred by news of the court hearings, a large queue formed outside 225 Piccadilly, where Saartjie performed as usual.

Sir Simon Le Blanc represented the African Institution. The aptly

named Edward Law, the first Baron Ellenborough, lord chief justice of England (appointed in 1802) and (significantly) a founding
member of the African Institution, presided as judge. Attorney General Sir William Garrow rose to make an application on behalf of
"this unfortunate female, who was exhibited to the public under circumstances of peculiar disgrace to a civilized country." His clients believed that the Hottentot Venus exhibition violated public decorum
and insulted human nature. The court, he urged, would learn that
the unfortunate female was brought unwillingly from her own country, kept in England for exhibition without her consent, and appeared compliant only as a result of the menaces and ill-treatment to
which she was constantly subjected. His clients wanted to liberate
Saartjie from her confinement, place her under proper protection
in England, and restore her to her country. No one could doubt that
the Hottentot Venus was kept in confinement, and his clients wished
Saartjie to know that she was not destitute of friends, and had the
support of men who were the friends of all humanity.

Flourishing the affidavits of Bullock, Macaulay, Babington, and
Van Wageninge, Garrow said that a writ of habeas corpus should be
issued on Saartjie's captors. Given, however, the particular circumstances of this situation, he suggested that bringing the Hottentot
Venus before them might offend both her sensibilities and the deli-
cacy of the court. Her keepers, Garrow continued, must demonstrate
why they should not be subject to the "Great Writ" of habeas corpus,
and must agree to allow Saartjie to be interviewed by "persons who
understood her language" without their being present.

Applying for a writ of habeas corpus, the African Institution followed established precedent on cases of the legality of slavery in England. Slaves were bought and displayed in the Elizabethan and Stuart
courts, advertised for sale through most of the eighteenth century,
and bequeathed in wills as late as the 1820s. However, Lord Chief
Justice Holt in the early eighteenth century opined that "as soon as a
Negro comes into England, he becomes free," and in 1762 the lord
chancellor stated that "as soon as a man puts foot on English ground,

he is free: a negro may maintain an action against his master for ill usage, and may have a Habeas Corpus, if restrained of his liberty."

It was Lord Mansfield's judgment in the case of James Somerset in 1772 that consolidated the use of habeas corpus in cases concerning illegal slavery. Led by Granville Sharp, this test case between the West India merchants and the abolitionists determined conclusively that slavery could not exist in England. Somerset, a slave brought from Virginia to England by his owner, escaped, but was then recaptured, bound in irons, and due to be shipped to Jamaica. The Court of the King's Bench issued a writ of habeas corpus on the ship's captain, requiring him to present Somerset to the court. Somerset's counsel, Serjeant-at-Law William Davys at the Court of the King's Bench, claimed that "England was too pure an Air for a Slave to breathe in." Macaulay's stirring rhetoric about Saartjie's right to breathe free air over England was a direct reference to the Somerset case.

Winning Saartjie's trust was essential. She might be justifiably suspicious and hostile to being made to appear, yet again, as a public spectacle, this time in an intimidating courtroom. Equally, the African Institution seemed afraid that the infamous Venus could not be relied upon to appear in court decently dressed. After all, as the affidavits attested, in her performance she appeared to be naked. At this, Lord Ellenborough raised his bushy eyebrows. "She is so tightly habited?" he asked. "Yes, My Lord, so as absolutely to appear as if she were naked," replied Sir William Garrow. "She is dressed in a colour as nearly resembling her skin as possible. The dress is contrived to exhibit the entire frame of her body, and the spectators are even desired to touch particular parts of her person."

Lord Ellenborough scanned the affidavit. "And does it state that she shews a feeling of pain from that circumstance? I do not call for what might be an indelicate exposure; but only desire to know if the mode of exhibition be such as to give pain to a sensitive mind." The court agreed that Saartjie's state of mind could only be discovered by interviewing her directly. On the question of whether the show was an offense to public decency, Le Blanc reminded the court, the defendants could only be made to answer this under a separate criminal charge.

Lord Ellenborough considered the question of Saartjie providing her own statement. "Is it ascertained that she speaks Dutch?" he asked Sir William Garrow, who confirmed that Cesars had stated that Saartjie understood "Low Dutch" (Afrikaans). Lord Ellenborough pursued, "Have you nobody who speaks what may be termed her own vernacular tongue?" It may not be easy to find such a native speaker, he suggested, but it was necessary, as the language in which her keeper had been heard to address Saartjie might be merely words of command, "a language which it is well known is easily taught." However, Macaulay made a mistake in his evidence when he asserted his suspicion "that Hendrik Cesars himself can only make her comprehend him by threats and signs." Macaulay did not realize that the Afrikaans (known also as Low or "kitchen" Dutch) in which Saartjie and Hendrik conversed fluently was in fact the indigenous language of slaves, servants, free blacks, and urban workers at the Cape. Macaulay was also mistaken when he said that he did "not think that there is in Europe a person who can make himself understood by the unfortunate object of the inquiry." As it turned out, there were in fact Afrikaans speakers in cosmopolitan London able to translate.

Macaulay was concerned that people might be misled by the deceptive "softness" of Saartjie's hands, and worried that "her being able to dance and to play on some sort of musical instrument, do not exactly coincide with the idea of her being a slave." Lord Ellenborough insisted that the court must ascertain directly from Saartjie herself whether or not she experienced "pain at the exposure to which she is subjected." The court then asked what would happen to Saartjie should it be established that she was in fact being detained in a state of slavery. When brought up under habeas corpus, Saartjie could go where she pleased, "and where," asked Simon Le Blanc, "is she to go?"

Sir William Garrow confirmed that there were persons "ready to take her, and she is to be told so." He moved that Saartjie be brought before the court "in order to declare from her own mouth whether

her present situation is voluntary or compelled." Le Blanc supported
Saartjie's right to self-determination: "She is to be left to judge for
herself."

Declaring that the court must come to know Saartjie's mind and
that it was interested only in her true situation, Lord Ellenborough
granted the rule:

> [I]t is ordered, that Tuesday next be given to Alexander Dun-
> lop and Hendrik Cesars, to shew cause why a writ of habeas
> corpus should not issue directed to them, commanding them
> to have the body of a certain native of South Africa, denomi-
> nated the Hottentot Venus, before the court immediately. . . .
> And it is further ordered, that one or two such person or per-
> sons as shall be approved for that purpose by the coroner and
> attorney, have free access to the said native of South Africa at
> the house of the said Alexander Dunlop and Hendrik Cesars
> in York Street Piccadilly, in the absence of the said Alexander
> Dunlop and Hendrick Cesars, but in the presence of one or
> two such persons as shall be nominated by them, and to be
> approved of by the said coroner and attorney for the purpose
> of conversing with her.

The case adjourned for the weekend.

USING THE PROFITS FROM THE SHOW, Dunlop and Cesars hired the
services of junior barrister Stephen Gaselee for their defense. Gaselee instructed them to make sure Saartjie had a proper business contract, and to ensure that the court could be persuaded that Cesars
had been removed from the exhibition.

Tuesday November 27, 1810, was a momentous day for Saartjie.

Dunlop took her to Sweeting's Alley to see Arend Jacob Guitard, a
Dutch-speaking public notary. Dunlop presented Guitard with an
agreement drawn up between Saartjie and himself, dated October
29, and asked him to translate it into Dutch, and then to read it out
to her and confirm that it was to her satisfaction. Crucially, the con-

tract began with the stipulation that it was backdated to March 20, 1810, the same day that Dunlop received permission from the governor's office, approved by Lord Caledon, to depart from the Cape, "together with his servant." Under her contract, "Saartjie Baartman," in addition to "performing such domestic duties as her master might reasonably demand of her," agreed to allow herself "to be viewed by the public of Ireland and England 'just as she was.' " Dunlop committed to pay all the expenses of the voyage, and to give Saartjie, in case of illness, "all the care and all such medicines as she might require," and "to defray the cost of repatriating her should she desire to return to her own country." Significantly, the contract covered Saartjie's key concerns: profit sharing, warmer clothes, better medical treatment, and the guarantee that she would be sent home. Guitard read Saartjie his translation "twice plainly and distinctly," and claimed to be satisfied that she understood the contents. Saartjie and Guitard then had a conversation. Was Saartjie contented with her situation, and did she have enough good food and drink? Yes, she replied to all his questions.

And this deponent also asked the said Saartjie Baartman whether she preferred either to return to the Cape of Good Hope or stay in England, and [to] that she replied—Stay here.

That same afternoon, five well-heeled eminences presented themselves at Saartjie's York Street lodgings. Dunlop and Cesars were forbidden to attend. Two Afrikaans-speaking merchants, Samuel Solly and John George Moojen, were translators for, respectively, the African Institution and Dunlop and Cesars. James Templer, coroner of the Court of the King's Bench, supervised the proceedings. Gaselee and Le Blanc represented their clients. The inquisitory procedure undertaken to interview Saartjie was thorough and scrupulous. The penalties for trifling with legal procedures were stringent, so everyone had to take care to relay truthfully what they observed and recorded.

Saartjie was interviewed in "Low" Dutch (Afrikaans), which, Solly and Moojen confirmed, "she perfectly understood." The conversation lasted for about three hours. This occasion inspired press myths that cast Saartjie in the role of destiny's controlling heroine. She appeared, it was rumored, "magnificently attired," offered her guests presents, and declared with great force that she came to and remained in England by her own free will and consent.

At the interview, Saartjie recounted her childhood and early life at the Cape. She came, she asserted, "by her own consent to England and was promised half of the money for exhibiting her person," for a period of six years; and, she claimed, "went personally to the government in company with Hendrik Cesars to ask permission to go to England." So saying, Saartjie presented her new contract. Mr. Dunlop, Saartjie explained, promised to pay for her to go home in six years' time, "the money belonging to her with her." In the meantime, she was "kindly treated," and apart from the fact that she needed warmer clothes, had no complaints. She had "no desire whatever of returning to her own country," and would rather stay in England "because she likes the country and has money given her by her master." She claimed that no personal violence or threats had been used against her, and stressed that she was treated modestly. Solly and Moojen were unconvinced:

> To the various questions we put to her whether if she chose at
> any time to discontinue her person being exhibited, she
> might do so, we could not draw a satisfactory answer from her.
> She understands very little of the agreement made with her by
> Mr Dunlop on the 29th October and which agreement she
> produced to us.

They were at pains to enter a specific concluding clause to the transcript of Saartjie's interview, stressing that "she could neither read nor write."

The court reconvened on Wednesday November 28. Stephen Gaselee opened on behalf of Dunlop and Cesars. He would show, he declared, that "Saartjie Baartman" (referred to by her own name for the first time in court) was neither kept under improper restraint, nor a slave brought unwillingly or illegally from the Cape. If, after he had presented the evidence, the court should still think that she was treated with "anything like cruelty," his clients, he assured the court, "were willing to give her up at once."

Gaselee, on whom Dickens based the irascible Justice Stareleigh (Bordell v. Pickwick), was "a skilful special pleader" who later became a judge (1824), received a knighthood (1825), and was vice president of the Royal Humane Society. Gaselee laid out the essence of his clients' defense. Since the African Institution lodged its affidavit on October 17, Mr. Dunlop had taken over the direction of Saartjie's exhibition from Mr. Cesars, due to the incident during which Cesars had allegedly intimidated Saartjie by raising his hand to her. Following this complaint, Cesars had "been removed from his situation" as master of ceremonies and with him, Gaselee implied, the threat of physical violence against her.

Gaselee addressed the court on the subject of slavery and the freedom of human beings in England. To emphasize her identity as free subject, he called Saartjie by her proper name. Saartjie was not, as slaves had been in the eighteenth century, an object of displayed merchandise exploitable for the profit of others, but a free woman who displayed herself willingly on condition that she receive a share of the profits from her exhibition. Gaselee could confirm from her own affidavit that she was promised her portion. So anxious were his clients to prove that Saartjie was not held under constraint but was a free agent contracted to perform, that they welcomed the interference of the court and would do anything to satisfy its demands.

In this spirit, his clients invited the African Institution to nominate and appoint a trustee to manage Saartjie's income and disburse her allowance and annuity, as they saw fit. This suggestion underlined the assumption of Saartjie's incapacity to manage her own income. Saartjie's right and understanding of how to make money was one thing, her ability to manage it, quite another. The African Institution declined the offer, as Gaselee suspected they would. Committed to defending public morality, they could not undertake to administer the profits of what they regarded as immoral earnings from entertainment that was, in their eyes, virtually prostitution.

Gaselee moved to the question of whether the Hottentot Venus exhibition was *contra bonos mores* (against good morals). Saartjie stated in her affidavit that there was nothing indecent about her appearance. The complaint that her "thin silk dress" was too revealing was inaccurate. It covered her body and underneath she wore "a covering of cotton." However, Saartjie had requested warmer clothes, and this demand would be met.

Gaselee presented to the attorney general the results of the interview with Saartjie, Dunlop's affidavit, and Saartjie's contract. This evidence brought the case to a legal but not moral resolution. Sir William Garrow conceded to Gaselee that Dunlop and Cesars had met the requirements of the court. Saartjie was "plainly not under restraint," and as she had given her own consent to be exhibited, the court could interfere no further. Moreover, he added in telling reference to Saartjie's assumed delinquency, if she were set at liberty "the only effect of taking her from her keepers would be to let her loose to go back again."

The case turned on the question of whether Saartjie had the right to sell herself, and whether, as a subordinated subject, she was capable of giving her consent to do so. In slavery, "the buyer gives nothing, the seller receives nothing." Saartjie had apparently agreed to a contract that guaranteed her an annual wage. From Elizabethan times, English legal precedent held that a person might enter into a contract of service for life, but not sell himself as a slave, as the rules governing servitude by contract would "not permit the servant to incorporate into his contract the ingredients of slavery." These judgments were intended to protect the liberty of individuals who wished to sell themselves, while preventing any possibility that a person might legitimately consent to become a slave. The distinction was crucial to the ideology of free-market labor. A person could sell his labor, though not himself, even if in receipt of his wages he remained perpetually dependent.

Rousseau would scoff. Consent was a myth disguising the fraud and coercion by which most of mankind were subordinated. No one except a lunatic would consent to their own bondage. But, as Garrow said, the application for the writ of habeas corpus could not be sustained now that Saartjie's sworn affidavit of contract and consent had been presented. The court agreed that Saartjie could voluntarily degrade herself for the price named, and the law interfere no further. Because she gave her labor willingly, she was deemed free, although clearly dependent.

In Saartjie's case the issues of contract and consent were complicated by the fact that she was protected by Lord Caledon's 1809 Proclamation on the registration and contracting into service of "Hottentots." Garrow pointed out that Cesars had registered Saartjie as a servant before a magistrate, but while "a free servant might leave the Cape . . . no Hottentot would be permitted to do so." Cesars had not applied for permission for her to leave the Cape. Lord Caledon was furious when he discovered for what purpose the contract had been made between Cesars and Saartjie. Lord Ellenborough interjected that certainly Lord Caledon knew nothing of Saartjie's illegal departure from South Africa, or he would have prevented it. "The matter," Lord Ellenborough pronounced disapprovingly, "was allowed by an interior person in office there." That "interior person" was the duped and scapegoated Henry Alexander, the governor's secretary.

Summing up his judgment, Lord Ellenborough cautioned Dunlop and Cesars to treat Saartjie well, or, he threatened, referring to the widely publicized incident of Cesars's public bullying, "the law would direct its arm with uplifted resentment against the offending parties." Supposed to be under restraint, Saartjie had "in express terms declared the reverse." It seemed that she had no desire of changing her situation or returning home immediately. Therefore, Dunlop and Cesars must pay her as contracted, and for "as long as she consented to the exhibition."

Closing the case, Lord Ellenborough offered the African Institution a recommendation for further action. "If there be any offence to decency in the exhibition that comes in another way:—that may be the ground of a prosecution." This was an invitation to the Clapham Sect to bring a charge of public indecency against Saartjie's exhibition. But they never did. To institute a private prosecution on grounds of indecency would have been difficult, costly, and risky.

The Clapham Sect romanticized Saartjie as a dispossessed child of Africa, fallen from a state of atavistic noble savagery to crude sexual, scientific exploitation in the modern factory of sin. In their eyes, she had no benefits from exile, and was entirely degraded by her display. At the outset of the trial they had sentimentalized Saartjie as a victim of Cesars and Dunlop's concupiscence; now they judged her a victim of her own concupiscence. Saartjie's response to the case brought on her behalf suggests a combination of naïve obstinacy with sanguine practicality. The white wigs might argue over whether she was slave or freewoman, but Saartjie knew that she was seller and commodity in one, and must take care of herself.

The abolitionists lost their case. Saartjie won herself a contract, written security of profit sharing, warmer clothes, and passage home. Business at 225 Piccadilly continued as usual.

Publicity generated by the case ensured the show's success for the duration of the winter. The press suggested that "Sartjee" had bested both the free-marketeers who exploited her and the abolitionists who sought to send her to Bible school. Saartjie now incarnated the belief that the former slave turned wage laborer was a free individual. Her "bright gold" and suggestively pendulous moneybags featured as motifs in many popular cartoons; Saartjie was depicted in fashionable European dress, an heiress besieged by fortune hunters. She was not seen as a sympathetic victim, but a dexterous businesswoman who had outmaneuvered her managers and made herself attractive to eligible bachelors as a woman of means.

In historical terms, the conclusion of Saartjie's case was a compromise in favor of free-market capitalism. Had she brokered for herself the best result possible, given the choices, or was she now doubly enslaved? When Saartjie said "Stay here" to Solly and Moojen, did she speak against her true wishes, as a prisoner under duress, and for

fear of reprisal from Dunlop and Cesars? She understood that the
men who had taken her managers to court offered release from exhibiting herself, and would send her home. Yet she regarded the
offer with suspicion. What did these men want in return for her
agreement? Macaulay and the abolitionists assumed Saartjie's desire
to return to South Africa. Yet it cannot be ignored that the outcome
of the case also suggests that Saartjie demanded the rights of the
working immigrant to be paid for her labor and enjoy, if only temporarily, the comparative benefits of exile.

In London, she was no longer just an ordinary, subjugated
Khoisan servant girl, but one of London's most recognizable figures,
who was promised wages beyond her expectations. It is sensible to as-
sume that Saartjie hoped and expected that she would ultimately return home. Most exiles do. But what, exactly, did she have to go back
to in Cape Town, apart from the certainty of continued drudgery
under white colonial rule, stirring the pot and raking ashes from the
fire of domestic servitude?

In the meantime, Saartjie had well-paid work and a bona fide contract to continue performing at 225 Piccadilly.

Chapter 8

CACHE-SEXE

O N TUESDAY APRIL 30, 1811, this announcement appeared in the London *Morning Post:*

> THE HOTTENTOT VENUS takes her FINAL DEPARTURE in a FEW WEEKS from this Metropolis, which accounts for the crowds of Fashionables, particularly of her own sex, who daily attend the Exhibition, the false idea of indelicacy being now entirely, and very properly, got over, from her having been visited as a truly interesting object of natural curiosity by some of the first Ladies of Distinction in the Kingdom. Her contour and formation certainly surpass any thing of the kind ever seen in Europe, or perhaps ever produced on the face of the earth. [Those] who have not seen this most wonderful uncommon creature, will lament their want of curiosity after her departure.

Saartjie's court case had boosted the show's popularity. In November 1810, a Christmas pantomime entitled *The Hottentot Venus: or Harlequin in Africa* opened to appreciative audiences in London, and afterwards toured the provinces. Saartjie's appearance in a deck of playing cards whose fifty-two subjects were chosen to typify London life in 1811 (she was shown singing and dancing before a beaming male audience) demonstrated her popularity.

A dramatic change in Dunlop's professional circumstances made the threesome entirely dependent on Saartjie's labor. Embarrassed by Dunlop's public exposure of Lord Caledon's maladministration, which had allowed Saartjie to depart South Africa illegally, Dunlop's military employers axed him; on December 25, 1810, he was placed on half-pay, with no prospect of a new posting.

Summer approached, the traditional touring season. Fairs, pleasure gardens, and outdoor amusements promised fresh audiences and lower overheads. The exhibition at 225 Piccadilly closed in May 1811, and for the next three years, until the summer of 1814, the Hottentot Venus toured Britain. Saartjie appeared in London, Brighton, and Bath. On August 28, 1811, the Reverend Halloran noted Saartjie's itinerant touring around the country, managed by Dunlop. Then, at the end of the year, she unexpectedly appeared in a cathedral.

On the cold morning of December 1, 1811, before a crammed Sunday congregation in the Collegiate and Parish Church of Christ in Manchester, Saartjie was baptized. The chaplain who christened her was the infamous Reverend Joshua Brookes, one of Anglican England's best-known priests. Brookes was almost as short as Saartjie, and the cathedral's ancient and imposing stone baptismal font was taller than them both. For twenty-two years she had been Saartjie Baartman from the Gamtoos River. On this Sunday, better heeled than any black working-class Mancunian, she entered the Christian church and was given a wholly Anglicized name: Sarah.

The 1811 baptismal register contains a uniquely detailed annotation:

> Sarah Bartmann, a Female Hottentot from the Colony of the
> Cape of Good Hope, born on the Borders of Caffraria, bap-
> tized this Day by Permission of the Lord Bishop of Chester in
> a Letter from his Lordship to Jos. Brookes Chaplain.

Because special permission was required from the bishopric to baptize a person who was not a local parishioner, Brookes wrote to the bishop of Chester, Bowyer Edward Sparke, laying out the situation. Sadly, this correspondence was destroyed when the cathedral was bombed during the Blitz.

The intrigued press reported Saartjie's christening, and specu-
lated as to "who were the sponsors of this extraordinary occasion."
On the following Saturday, Saartjie collected her baptismal certificate, signed by her sponsor, Dunlop. She remained visible in the
press, politics, and popular culture, but the real Saartjie disappeared
almost entirely from public view, suggesting that her baptism was
precipitated by an important development in her personal life, of
which there is no record. Perhaps she was pregnant, planning to get
married, or both. However, it is questionable why a press so eager to
remark on Saartjie's baptism would not leap upon the opportunity to
report her wedding.

In April 1812 Saartjie appeared in Ireland, performing for five
days in the city of Limerick, where, "much to the credit of the people," she "was visited by very few." That she was on show four months
after her baptism does not rule out the possibility that she was pregnant, and subsequently gave birth to a second child. If she did have
a second baby at this time, it never became public knowledge. There
has been speculation that Saartjie and Dunlop married, but no evidence to support this supposition has yet been found.

Saartjie reemerged in Portsmouth in the summer of 1812, at Dunlop's bedside. On July 18, Dunlop died, of unknown causes, freeing
Saartjie and Cesars from their dependency on him. Dunlop's military pension ceased on his death, and he appeared to have no remaining contact with family. It seems that he left whatever he had to
Cesars and Saartjie. Lord Ellenborough had made Dunlop guaran-
tor of Saartjie's contract. With his death, she lost her only legal surety
that she would get home.

From July 1812, Saartjie disappeared for two years without trace.
These were her last years of anonymity. In 1814 Saartjie reappeared,
in a blaze of publicity; thenceforward she would remain permanently
in the public gaze, for two centuries.

SHORTLY AFTER THE ALLIES took back Paris on March 30, 1814,
Saartjie and Cesars (the latter traveling under the rather feeble alias
of "Henry Taylor") boarded the mail coach to Dover, struck out by

boat from under its chalk cliffs across the slate gray channel, and headed towards Paris into the eye of a historical storm.

Whatever had happened to Saartjie in the intervening period, she entered France without a child, or a husband. Cesars adopted an alias because Lord Ellenborough's ruling removed him from direct management of Saartjie, and the city was full of gossiping English. When Saartjie and Cesars arrived in Paris in the summer of 1814, slavery and the slave trade were still legal in France and her dominions.

Saartjie arrived in France in the wake of the final allied effort against Napoleon. The allies, led by Tsar Alexander, took Paris on the last day of March. Napoleon abdicated four days later, Talleyrand led the vote in the French Senate for the return of the Bourbons, Louis XVIII was restored, and Napoleon left Fontainebleau for Elba.

Amid this tide of eminent men moving in and out of Paris was Georges Léopold Chrétien Cuvier, Europe's foremost scientist. As Saartjie's coach rolled into central Paris that summer of 1814, the Mammoth, as he was nicknamed, dominated the Musée National d'Histoire Naturelle (National Museum of Natural History). The museum was situated amid the trees of the Jardin des Plantes and its exotic zoo of wild animals, presided over by Étienne Geoffroy Saint-Hilaire. Saartjie would soon be at the epicenter of the debate about race and the human species that raged between these two men, an intellectual battle described by Goethe as "the most important event in European history."

Saartjie and Cesars took lodgings at 15 Rue Neuve des Petits Champs (now the Rue des Petits Champs), parallel to the north end of the Palais Royal gardens, amid the terraced streets, glittering arcades, and white colonnades of the Palais Royal, Paris's theater district and mecca for amusements. The building at 15 Rue Neuve des Petit Champs had a well-known exhibition hall on the ground floor and accommodation above. The address had been home to many of the Palais Royal's leading attractions.

Situated at the heart of political Paris, the wrought iron balconies of Saartjie's new home looked out over flagstones paved with the republican libertine tradition, a heady mixture of sex, knowledge, blood, and freedom. The city was energized by the demobilization hysteria of the Restoration. Just across the river on the left bank the buildings of the Museum of Natural History sat among the lush palms, pink flamingos, and baying wolves of the Jardin des Plantes, recently renamed the Jardin du Roi following the defeat of Napoleon.

On September 10, Professor André Thouin, administrator of the Museum of Natural History, received a letter from a certain Henry Taylor, containing an invitation to a private view at 15 Rue Neuve des Petits Champs on Tuesday the thirteenth. Attached to the letter was a poster engraving of Saartjie, who, it explained, was a member of the Hottentot tribe from the borders of the Gamtoos River in the African interior. The letter stressed Saartjie's interest as an object of natural history to the informed observer. Before the opening of the exhibition to the public, Mr. Taylor offered an exclusive preview of this person and her "conformation singulière" to the museum's professors.

This letter was read to the weekly board meeting of the museum on Wednesday the fourteenth, the day after the private view, and passed over in favor of the more urgent matter of the impending visit by the new governor of the Cape, Lord Charles Henry Somerset. The board resolved to ask the new governor for typical animals of South Africa for the menagerie. Étienne Geoffroy Saint-Hilaire, Georges Cuvier, and Henri Marie Ducrotay de Blainville were the leading members of the twelve-strong professorial board of the Museum of Natural History. Intellectual descendants of Buffon, Lamarck, and Linnaeus, these men constituted the world's premier team of scientific naturalists. The board took no action on the letter from "Mr. Taylor," but Cuvier particularly noted its contents.

Georges Cuvier, born in 1769, had bright, penetrating blue eyes, thick, wavy red hair, heavy features, and an aptitude for survival. He was short, his walk ponderous and slow, and he was often disheveled. Lean during the Revolutionary years, he filled out during the Empire and after the Restoration "grew enormously fat," to the point that he avoided bending over, for fear of an attack of apoplexy.

By 1814 Cuvier held the Professional Chair for Comparative Anatomy at the Museum of Natural History, and the Chair of Natural History at the Collège de France, the world's largest scientific research establishment. He had risen to fame as Citizen Cuvier of the revolutionary state, prospered under Napoleon as a member of the governing elite, and then inveigled himself into the good favor of the new monarchy with such convincing, and newly revealed, anti-revolutionary convictions as to be made chancellor of the University of Paris, and councillor of state to the king.

Despite hagiographic versions of Cuvier, he was in reality a plodding, assiduous creep and physical coward, who owed his ascendance to the fact that he never undertook the adventurous risks of fieldwork, unlike his mentor, colleague, and rival, Saint-Hilaire. Ultimately, Cuvier prevailed, but he was paranoid, lonely, self-pitying, and constantly besieged by imaginary monsters threatening to assail his intellectual preeminence. Cuvier's primacy proved disastrous for Saartjie.

On Sunday, September 18, Cesars placed an advertisement in the *Journal de Paris* announcing the opening of the exhibition:

The HOTTENTOT VENUS, recently arrived from London. Now on show to the public at 15, Rue Neuve des Petits Champs. This extraordinary phenomenon is the only member of the Hauzanana tribe ever to have appeared in Europe. In this woman, as extraordinary as she is surprising, the public has a perfect example of this tribe, which inhabits the most southerly parts of Africa. The Hottentot Venus differs greatly in character from her people, ordinarily most surly, in her sweetness, graciousness and winning ways. She wears all those ornaments that on holidays are used as ceremonial finery by the tribe to which she belongs. One may obtain at the same place an engraving of the Hottentot Venus, taken from life. Entry 3 fr.

Saartjie was marketed, once again, as being both typical and unique. She captured the essence of contemporary Parisian entertainment:

a compound of science, phantasmagoria, fantasy, and curiosity. Saartjie was unknown when she arrived in London in 1810, but when she reached Paris in 1814, she was a recognized icon whose reputation as scantily clad totem goddess preceded her. Rumored nudity, flaunted buttocks, and curling pipe smoke had become her trademarks, and there was gossip that she was a courtesan, or a prostitute. These were stage fictions. She had never yet appeared naked onstage, her bottom was, granted, impressive, but far from unusual in the mere fact of being substantial. The pipe was a prop. Saartjie must have dissipated many hours of boredom blowing smoke into the eyes of her fascinated audience, contemplating the spectacular idiocy and casual cruelty of the people who paid to stare at her.

Now that she only had Cesars to look after, Saartjie's household duties were lighter. Each was the other's meal ticket, and the duo was more than ever firmly bound by the mutual tyranny of master and servant. A transformation came over Saartjie in Paris. She became overwhelmingly amiable and ebullient onstage, and joked with her audience in Dutch and English. She danced with energy, and her singing in "her own mother-tongue" charmed the Parisian critics. This behavior was ambiguous: was Saartjie genuinely cheerful, or was her exuberant jollity a mask for misery? Freed of Dunlop, she had a fuller share of her earnings, and the novelty of a new, warmer foreign city. Possibly she had a new lover; there were unsubstantiated press reports that she married in Paris. Yet Saartjie's greater engagement with her audiences heightened rather than lessened her aura of loneliness and isolation, and it suggested an increasingly cognac-fueled desperation at the realization that her circumstances were inescapable. Through her travels she had discovered the boundlessness of servitude for the poor and unfree.

Saartjie worked her shift from noon till six, and spent the evenings at restaurants, bars, and cafés drumming up further business, or going by private invitation to dinners, parties, and salons at "charming" houses. After a day of being ogled and prodded on the boards, Saartjie was subjected to the prurient curiosity of her European sisters, denizens of polite society. At one supper party in the

Palais Royal, Saartjie's entrance caused hysteria among the ladies, who rushed away from her, apparently terrified, "and huddled behind the curtains." Observing this reaction, Saartjie was "plunged . . . into a sudden fit of melancholy." She bowed her head, and tears fell from her eyes. Her pathetic vulnerability reassured, perhaps even shamed, the cowering women. They ventured from behind the curtains and approached her, holding her hands, fingering her necklaces, and touching her clothes. Following so fast on their fear and rejection, the objectifying curiosity displayed in this sudden, uninvited physical intimacy must have been almost unendurable for Saartjie.

Satirists cast Saartjie in the role of Paris's favorite noble-savage savant. Looking at Parisian society with an apparently natural outsider's eye, Saartjie was portrayed, once again, as the topical stranger, commenting with innocent wit on the excesses of Restoration society, arbitrating on fashion, remarking on the manners of French and English women, and on the relations between the sexes.

On November 19 a one-act play entitled *The Hottentot Venus: or the Hatred of Frenchwomen* opened at the Vaudeville Theatre. Written by Messrs. Théaulon de Lambert, Dartois, and Brazier, with a score of no less than thirty-four musical numbers, the show borrowed the plot of Vadé's *La Canadienne* (The Canadian Girl), and starred a popular young actress, Mlle Rivière. Adolphe, a young baronet-to-be and victim of two fickle French wives, inspired by traveler's tales, resolves to marry "une femme sauvage" whom he can count on to be free of civilized vices. Adolphe is encouraged by his uncle, the Baron, a bluff traveler who assures him that "Frenchwomen are the most beautiful in the world, except for American Indian Squaws and Hottentot girls."

Adolphe's cousin Amélie, secretly in love with him, dresses herself up "in gorgeous Hottentot costume," pretends to speak only untranslatable "Hottentot," and inveigles the smitten Adolphe into a betrothal. Amélie is unmasked when a chevalier who is in love with her dramatically unrolls a print of the real Hottentot Venus whose show he has just seen in Paris. At the sight of her portrait, "everyone gives a cry of terror," and Adolphe's desire for a barbarian bride is instantly exorcised. He marries Cousin Amélie, and conventional white, heterosexual order is restored. The show was an instant box-office hit. Reviewers compared Mlle Rivière with Saartjie, disparaging the original: "There is more than one difference between Mlle Rivière and her foreign model. A young and pretty actress like herself can have no relation to a *savage Venus*."

French audiences feared and adored Saartjie for her difference. It was an idolatrous kind of love, infused with unapologetic French exoticism. "When it comes to blacks, the imagination of white folks is something else," Josephine Baker would observe when she performed in Paris a century later. The original Hottentot Venus might have concurred. Saartjie's popular image in England was one of wiliness, stoical obstinacy, and opportunistic pragmatism. In France, she metamorphosed into a tragic heroine and showgirl manqué, a fallen goddess of love, and the epitome of the African exotic.

Despite the success of the show, Saartjie and Cesars struggled to cope with life in Paris. They spoke little French, and Cesars's contacts were poor. He had promised his wife that he would return after five years. His time was nearly up, but he had yet to make his fortune. At the end of October he extended Saartjie's daily show times from six to a punishing ten hours, to maximize profits. Performing daily from eleven in the morning to nine o'clock at night took its toll on Saartjie's health, and by the end of the year she was suffering from exhaustion, recurrent flu, and the deleterious effects of the brandy she drank to keep going through her performances, private viewings, and late-evening displays at cafés and restaurants. Gradually, her ailments mutated into alcohol-related illnesses.

It is possible that Cesars drove her on with the incentive of raising sufficient funds for their joint passage home. Even if she believed him, the enticements for Saartjie to return home were ambiguous. Return to Cape Town meant that she could stop performing like a circus turn for the insatiable European audiences and take up again her life as domestic servant in the Cesars household. It wasn't much of a choice.

Buoyed by the obsession of novelty-driven Paris with the Hottentot Venus phenomenon, show takings were good in the run up to the
end of 1814. But when the new year began with Saartjie too ill to perform, Cesars panicked.

The year 1815 was eventful and calamitous. On the evening of
March 20 Napoleon reentered Paris, and was carried up the steps of
the Tuileries by a frenzied crowd. A frightened Louis XVIII had fled
down the same steps the night before, on his way to Ghent. (He
would return, exactly one hundred days later, following Napoleon's
defeat at Waterloo.) By October, the former Republican emperor
would be banished to the mournful, storm-beaten volcanic rock of
St. Helena, the prison island en route to Cape Town.

While Saartjie was offstage languishing in bed with the flu in January 1815, a predatory showman named Réaux, who had followed her
success, sensed opportunity and offered to take over *la Vénus Hottentote*
from Cesars. There is no record of the deal struck. Cesars returned
to Cape Town shortly thereafter. It is certain that Cesars profited
from the sale of Saartjie's exhibition rights. When he died in 1841 he
left his wife an inheritance of "two thousand ryks dollars pure." Re-
vising their will, the newly widowed Anna Catharina appointed Pieter
Cesars her universal heir, suggesting that their adopted daughter
had died, or become estranged. Thus, through a grim twist of fate,
Pieter Cesars, the man who originally took Saartjie from her Gamtoos River Valley home to Cape Town, inherited the remainder of the
wealth earned from her exploitation.

Together for so long, Saartjie and Cesars parted company as
swiftly as the turning of the tide. Saartjie was on her own, and had
learned too late the fundamental Faustian law of show business con-
tracts. Her emotional distress at Cesars's departure was evident. Her
characteristic stoicism crumbled; she wept in public, began to describe herself to strangers as unfortunate, and drank more and more
brandy.

Saartjie's return to the stage following her illness at a new venue
on the Rue Montesquieu was announced on January 22, 1815. "The
Hottentot Venus has changed owner," the press reported, asserting,

with no evidence, that Saartjie's new manager, Réaux, was also now her husband. Réaux was a shady figure. Described disingenuously in official correspondence with the Museum of Natural History as merely "a householder of Paris," he was in fact an entertainer and animal trainer with close connections to Paris's naturalists and scientists. Réaux lived with a small menagerie at 7 Cour des Fontaines (now Place de Valois), a courtyard directly opposite the east side of the Jardin du Palais Royal. It was to this address that Saartjie moved following Cesars's departure.

Monkey chatter, parrot squawks, and a chorus of constant rustling and scratching could be heard in the cobbled courtyard outside Réaux's apartment windows. The scientists nearby at the Museum of Natural History, keepers of their own much larger bestiary in the Jardin des Plantes, feigned disinterest in Réaux's populist occupations, yet knew him well; he served as one of the museum's network of animal resurrectionists, who, in exchange for cash, delivered small furry bodies in sacks for dissection and addition to the museum's growing natural history collection.

Although Saartjie was barely recovered from her illness, Réaux reopened the Hottentot Venus exhibition with an extended show time, a grueling twelve-hour shift from eleven in the morning to eleven at night. To promote the revival, Réaux ran a daily press campaign for over a fortnight, and announced new public perambulations of the Venus around Paris, for which he would give twenty-four hours' advance notice.

Réaux also began to speculate on other means of earning revenue from Saartjie's display. Taking advantage of his connections with the Museum of Natural History, he hatched a ghastly scheme. Without her consent, Réaux prepared the way for a performance that would make him a small fortune, and ultimately cost Saartjie her life.

Chapter 9
PAINTED FROM THE NUDE

IN EARLY SPRING 1815, a few days after the news reached Paris that Napoleon was marching on the capital, Saartjie made her way through the verdant chestnut and plane trees in the Jardin du Roi on the left bank. By arrangement between Réaux and the professorial board of the National Museum of Natural History, Saartjie was on her way to pose for three days as a life model for a panel of scientists and artists.

Prompted by Cesars's letter to the board, Cuvier went to see The Hottentot Venus, and asked Réaux to arrange a meeting after the show. The Mammoth was fascinated, and talked to Saartjie at length, promptly replenishing her quickly finished drinks. He recorded that she was cheerful and conversational; and, he noted, she drank spirits to excess.

The French scientific community had been following Saartjie's career since her arrival in Paris. In October 1815, the circle of savants based at the great chemist Claude-Louis Berthollet's country-house research institute at Arcueil, just outside of Paris, discussed Saartjie at a dinner gathering. Sir Charles Blagden, former secretary of the Royal Society and right-hand man to Joseph Banks, remarked in his diary, "Talk about the Hottentot Venus, before the girls; kept within the bounds of decency." A further entry in January 1815 describes "much talk" between these men about "Hottentots," and the question of whether "it's the Bosjeman women only who have the apron" and "the large posteriors." Jean-Claude Mertrud, professor of com-

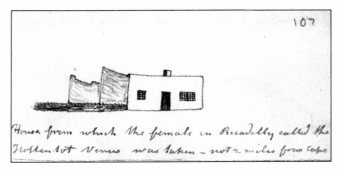

House from which the female in Piccadilly called the Hottentot Venus was taken – not 2 miles from Cape

Saartjie's Cape Town cottage, from a sketchbook by John Campbell, 1815. CAPE TOWN ARCHIVES REPOSITORY

Nursemaid suckling child by Lady Anne Barnard, Cape Town, 1798. NATIONAL LIBRARY OF SOUTH AFRICA

Panorama of Cape Town and harbor in the late eighteenth century by Johannes Schumacher. CAPE TOWN ARCHIVES REPOSITORY

Far left: Soldier of the Khoisan regiment by Lady Anne Barnard. CAPE TOWN ARCHIVES REPOSITORY

Left: Watercolor painting of Cape Colony Khoisan soldier in proposed regimental uniform, with tiger-skin helmet, 1808. THE NATIONAL ARCHIVES IMAGE LIBRARY, LONDON

Portrait of England's leading actor, John Philip Kemble, by M. A. Shee, RA, London, April 1803. NATIONAL PORTRAIT GALLERY, LONDON

Portrait of William Bullock from 1812, published in Rowley's *Ornithological Miscellany* in 1877. BRITISH LIBRARY

Bullock's Museum in 1810, 22 Piccadilly, London, described at the time by *Bell's Weekly Messenger* as "the most fashionable place of amusement in London." BRITISH MUSEUM

THE DEFORMITO-MANIA.

"The Deformito-mania," *Punch.*

Satirical engraving of Miss Ridsdale, "Sartjee," and Miss Harvey by William Heath, 1810, parodying three famous London courtesans—Henriette Dubochet, her sister Fanny, and her friend Julia Johnstone—who were known at the time as "The Three Graces." British Museum

Colored acquatint by Frederick Christian Lewis, advertising the Hottentot Venus. This poster was published by Hendrik Cesars on September 18, 1810.

Museum Africa, Johannesburg

Colored acquatint by Frederick Christian Lewis, published in March 1811, shortly before Saartjie went on tour. British Museum

A Crowded Street in London, by George Cruikshank, 1812, showing the bustling intensity of London life and its popular entertainments. Note the shopfront poster advertising "The Hottentot Venus" show. <small>WELLCOME LIBRARY, LONDON</small>

Satirical engraving by William Heath, November 1810. Lord Grenville, dressed as the Hottentot Venus, grasps Saartjie's hand. Behind Grenville stands his brother, the Marquis of Buckingham, and behind Saartjie, Lord Temple, Buckingham's son. <small>BRITISH MUSEUM</small>

Political cartoon by William Heath, 1810. Saartjie stands rump to rump with Lord Grenville whilst playwright Richard Brinsley Sheridan kneels behind and measures her bottom.

Caricature engraving by Charles Williams from 1811, published in 1822, satirizing the notion of an association between the Hottentot Venus and eros. With its plump white baby Cupid carried by Saartjie, the image inadvertently alludes to Saartjie's past as a domestic servant and nursemaid in a racially divided society.

Heroes of the Slave Trade Abolition by an unknown artist, showing Zachary Macaulay, leading abolitionist and founder of the African Institution, who led the battle to plead the cause of "that wretched object advertised and publicly shewn [*sic*] for money— the Hottentot Venus."

Cartoon by Charles Williams, December 1811, depicting the Duke of Clarence proposing to Saartjie. A notorious fortune hunter, the Duke had been famously turned down by at least nine heiresses, and at the time of the cartoon was averaging about one unsuccessful marriage proposal per month.

Political cartoon by Charles Williams depicting Saartjie and Lord Grenville going into business together, shortly after her court case, London, December 1810. Behind Grenville are Perceval, Chancellor of the Exchequer, Foreign Secretary Wellesley, Home Secretary Ryder, and Lord Chancellor Eldon. BRITISH MUSEUM

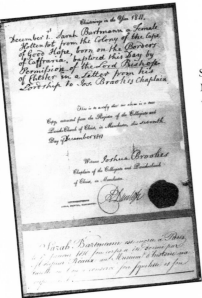

Saartjie's baptism certificate, Manchester, December 1811, which was found among her effects when she died in Paris on Friday, December 29, 1815 (note how it has been folded small for carrying).

MUSÉE DE L'HOMME

Engraving of Georges
Cuvier by Bernard Faye
Bernard.

FAYE—M.N.H.N.
(MUSEUM NATIONAL D'HISTOIRE
NATURELLE)

Cartoon by George Loftus, Paris, 1814. MUSEUM AFRICA, JOHANNESBURG

Satirical cartoon of the exhibition of Bonaparte's carriage at Bullock's Museum by Thomas Rowlandson, showing poster of Saartjie Baartman next to Napoleon's bust and a playbill of popular midget Count Boruwlaski, January 1816. BRITISH MUSEUM

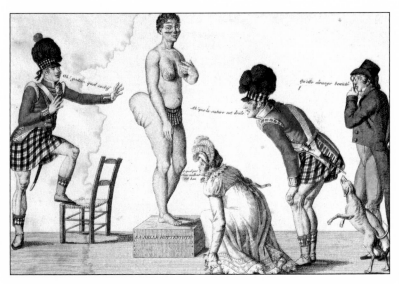

Unattributed cartoon, Paris, 1814, showing what Parisians regarded as another "curiosity"—Scots Guards, serving in the allied army of occupation. MUSEUM AFRICA, JOHANNESBURG

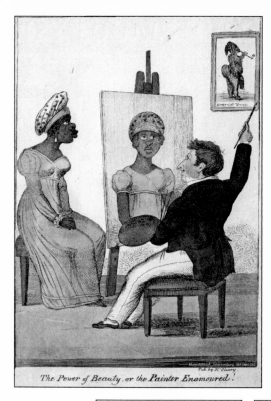

The Power of Beauty, or the Painter Enamoured!

Colored engraving by an unknown artist from 1827. On the wall hangs a portrait of Saartjie, who was still inspiring artists more than a decade after her death.

MUSEUM AFRICA, JOHANNESBURG

Right: Portrait by Nicolas Huet, Paris, March 1815.

MUSEUM AFRICA, JOHANNESBURG

Far right: Portrait by Léon de Wailly, Paris, March 1815.

MUSEUM AFRICA, JOHANNESBURG

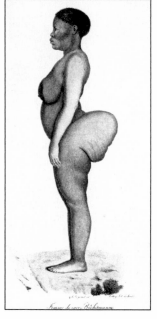

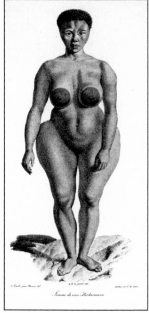

Colored engraving and genital cartouche of Jean-Baptiste Berré's original showing Saartjie naked, published in 1819 in the *Journal Complementaire du Dictionaire des Sciences Medicales.*

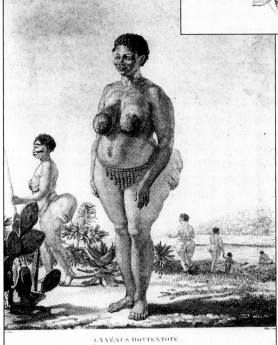

LA VÉNUS HOTTENTOTE.

Portrait by Jean-Baptiste Berré showing Saartjie covered, Paris, March 1815.

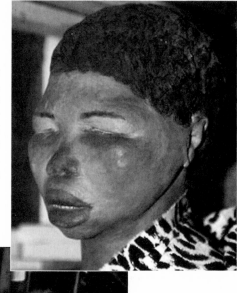

The head of Cuvier's full body cast of Saartjie, kept in the Musée de l'Homme from her death in 1815 and returned to South Africa in 2002.

TRACE IMAGES/REUTERS

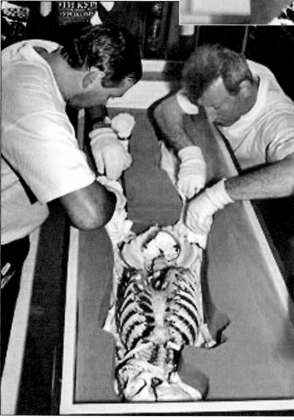

Museologists at the Musée de l'Homme pack Saartjie's skeleton for return to South Africa.

TRACE IMAGES/REUTERS

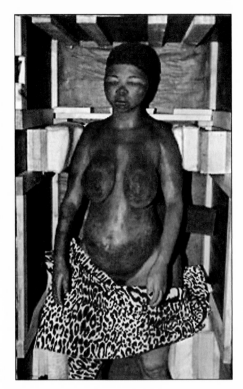

Saartjie's full body cast, taken at the time of her death, crated for transportation from France to South Africa in 2002.

TRACE IMAGES/REUTERS

Zapiro cartoon from *The Sowetan*, May 2, 2002, when Saartjie's remains were returned to South Africa. JONATHAN SHAPIRO

Saartjie's state funeral, Hankey, Eastern Cape,
August 9, 2002.

OBED ZILWA/TRACE IMAGES/REUTERS

parative anatomy at the Museum of National History and the Zoo, said that he much admired Cuvier's opinions on this subject.

Cuvier's protégé, Henri de Blainville, assistant professor at the Académie des Sciences, was also eager to scrutinize Saartjie. A panel was put together comprising zoologists, naturalists, anatomists, physiologists, illustrative artists, and draftsmen. Leading the scientific group were the formidable triumvirate of Saint-Hilaire, Cuvier, and de Blainville.

On February 16, Saint-Hilaire wrote to Monsieur Boucheseiche, head of the Paris police, requesting authorization to bring Saartjie to the Jardin du Roi for examination by the academicians. Her manager Réaux, Saint-Hilaire assured Boucheseiche, had given undertakings to act with discretion to preserve the public order. Réaux requested a report from the scientists, which he could use as further credentials for Saartjie's exhibition.

Saartjie passed by the caged animals in the museum zoo on her way to being examined, drawn, and painted by the foremost natural scientists of Europe. Several of the animals, such as the zebra and gnu, were gifts from governors of the Cape.

STANDING ON A PLATFORM in the atelier, her arm resting on a chair, Saartjie looked down at the men, their eyes sharp and bright with curiosity, looking up at her. Notebooks, sketchbooks, inkstands, pens, charcoal, eyeglasses, and a host of strange instruments bestrewed the lamplit room. Stoves burned the chill off the spring morning.

Cuvier, de Blainville, and Saint-Hilaire led the scientific team. All three specialized in comparative anatomy and zoology. A sort of early-nineteenth-century Indiana Jones, Saint-Hilaire had joined Napoleon's Egyptian campaign and enjoyed three years of high-risk scientific adventures amid the pyramids, collecting skulls and artifacts, studying the crocodiles of the Nile, and pursuing his fascination with the art of snake charming. During Saint-Hilaire's absence, Cuvier superseded him as France's leading naturalist. On his return, Saint-Hilaire pursued his research on genetic exaggerations and

comparative embryology. Contesting the notion that physical freak-
ery was a quirk of fate, he argued that physical aberrations explained
normal development. In so doing, he founded the science of teratology: the study of monstrosities or abnormal formations in animals
and plants.

The other members of the Académie des Sciences present included the physiologist Pierre Flourens, and Cuvier's brother
Frédéric, keeper of the menagerie. Cuvier's research assistants were
on hand to administer to their mentors and provide Saartjie with refreshments.

The museum had its own in-house team of staff painters. Resident
artist Léon de Wailly was professor of drawing at the Conservatoire
Royal des Arts et des Métiers. Specializing in quadrupeds and birds,
he painted for the museum's visual archive those living animals
"where no likeness exists." Nicolas Huet and Jean-Baptiste Berré produced hundreds of watercolor illustrations of flora and fauna, as well
as anatomical drawings for the museum's professors, working alongside the famous Redouté brothers, whose delicate and beautiful
drawings of plants were regarded as the aesthetic pinnacle of botanical illustration and flower painting. The work of Huet, de Wailly,
and Berré was both integral to the scientific project, and collectible
popular art. Color prints and posters of their paintings were reproduced and sold in great quantity all over Paris.

None of these artists, however, usually painted human subjects.

On the first day of her examination, Saartjie arrived in her stage
costume, as she believed the occasion required. Getting togged up in
this outfit took considerable effort, yet as Saartjie arranged herself
for the viewing, her observers seemed disconcerted. The source of
their dissatisfaction soon became clear. They expected her to pose
naked. A battle ensued in which Saartjie, object of the moment, attempted heroically to hold her ground. She argued with them, ignored their entreaties, and refused to remove a single item of her
ensemble.

Henri de Blainville made it clear that the scientists, anatomists,
physiologists, and artists gathered to examine *la Vénus Hottentote* dis-

tanced themselves, as intellectual men of art and science, from any interest in Saartjie's talents:

> As for what she had clearly learnt from Europeans, in order to exercise her trade, such as dancing . . . accompanying herself with skill on the tambourine, playing the Jew's harp, making certain gestures which one supposed to be of prayer, or her numerous and hideous grimaces . . . this [is] of little interest to naturalists.

De Blainville's dismissive suggestion that Saartjie merely mimicked her cultural accomplishments "from Europeans" was a cultural and racial insult.

What intrigued Saartjie's surveyors was the prospect of the close-up view of the legendary somatic attributes of a Khoisan woman. In five years of public performance, Saartjie had never appeared nude. Always covered by her skin-colored fleshings, her fur-trimmed silk-stockinged body had suggested without revealing; deforming the dreams of viewers, stimulating the curiosity and prurient surmise of those who had seen her, in person or print. Whether she was physical fact or theatrical fiction was a mystery popular audiences had to decide for themselves. Such theatrical ambiguity was, however, anathema to the great modern scientific classifiers of the world. Self-appointed arbiters of the imagination, they would discover what was fact about Saartjie Baartman, and vanquish fiction. For them to achieve this objective, the Hottentot Venus needed to be naked. Ribbons, feathers, beads, stockings, fur cape, headdress, carefully applied makeup, musical instruments, accessories, intimate garments; everything but her chewing tobacco had to go.

Saartjie was furious and appalled. The examination, formulated as an exercise in controlled scientific objectivity, was held up by protracted negotiations with her over her stubborn unwillingness to undress. By dint of courteous modesty, Saartjie had found a way to subvert the proceedings. The extent to which her attitude affected the entire event is reflected in de Blainville and Cuvier's scientific

lectures. Both men were forced to dedicate a large part of these research papers to the very unscientific subject of describing the problems caused by Saartjie's intractability on the point of removing her
clothes.

In classical legend Venus dominated hearts and minds largely by
means of her famous girdle. Imbued with mystical powers, this
unique raiment had the power to excite love and rekindle passion,
and granted the model beauty, grace, and elegance when worn even
by the most deformed. This powerful accessory enabled Juno to gain
the attentions of Jupiter, and helped Venus to subdue Vulcan's jeal-
ousy of her manifold infidelities. Elaborating this classical theme,
European travelers attributed to Khoisan women the legendary
"Hottentot apron," a pinafore of flesh supposed to conceal the "Hottentot" female's *mons Veneris*. While Greek goddesses wore magical
detachable corsetry, nobly savage Venuses, subdued to servitude,
had—according to travel accounts—natural "aprons," concealing
their fecund genitalia and eroticizing their alien appearance and
subjection.

Many European male travelers colluded in this collective fantasy.
A debate raged for 250 years as to whether the legendary "Hottentot
apron" resulted from nature or culture. When Captain James Cook
stopped at Cape Town on his way home in March 1771, he confided
to his diary that he intended to use the opportunity to explore "the
great question among natural historians, whether the women of this
country have or have not that fleshy flap or apron which has been
called the *Sinus pudoris*." Those favoring the natural explanation
dubbed the supposed condition with the pseudoscientific description of hypertrophy of the labia minora, and seized on the apron as
the clinching evidence that South Africa's much-debated indigenous
people were in fact fundamentally a different species from Europeans. It was only a short step from here to positing that "Hottentots"
were the missing link in the chain of being between humans and animals, and therefore essentially bestial in nature.

Others disagreed, arguing for the notional Hottentot *tablier* as a
form of cultural genital manipulation best understood as a fashion,

designed (depending on the commentator) to stimulate or repel erotic desire. As early as 1640 Nicolaus de Graaf described the resulting bodily "ornament" as "short thongs hanging down, cut from the body." François Le Vaillant, friend of Cuvier and fellow member of the Société des Observateurs de l'Homme, the world's first anthropological society, determined to recast the "Hottentot" as Africa's noble savage. He also strongly proposed a cultural rather than natural explanation for the "famous apron." It was, Le Vaillant claimed with paternalistic indulgence, a rather excessive, absurd foible of fashion, designed to cover women's genitals and neutralize desire.

Cuvier and de Blainville were thoroughly versed in these debates. Cuvier was a founder member of the Société des Observateurs de l'Homme, established in 1799. Using firsthand reports from their friends and historical travel accounts, these men hoped to discover for themselves the nature of this mantle of modesty.

But Saartjie had neither a magical girdle nor a "Hottentot apron." She had only a handkerchief.

It was the Mammoth who finally persuaded Saartjie to yield and remove her clothes. He and de Blainville competed to secure this concession. Saartjie's body became the territory battled over in their escalating struggle for preeminence. Furious, miserable, and exposed, Saartjie sought to retain her dignity with her little handkerchief.

De Blainville found Saartjie gentle and shy, charming when she liked someone, stubborn and contrary when she did not. Saartjie's modesty and her evident dislike of de Blainville proved great obstacles to his scientific enterprise:

> She appears to know shame, or there was at least a great deal
> of difficulty in persuading her to allow herself to be seen
> naked, and she was almost unwilling to discard, for a moment,
> the handkerchief with which she hid her sexual organs. All
> the more then, was it impossible to obtain permission from
> her to make an adequate examination of them.

Exasperated, de Blainville resorted to barefaced bribery. Saartjie, offended, refused. Much to Cuvier's satisfaction and amusement,
Saartjie "conceived a kind of hatred for M. de Blainville." In addition
to his pestering, de Blainville made himself ridiculous to Saartjie by
the contorted positions he assumed in his attempts to try and find
empirical evidence of her "Hottentot apron":

> In ordinary position, that is to say in upright posture, one cer-
> tainly sees no sign of any kind of pedicule formed by the labia
> majora . . . and even less any projection of the labia minora;
> but in certain positions, as for example when Saartjie bent
> down, or even when she walked, on looking from behind one
> could see hanging between the thighs a fleshy appendage of
> at least an inch in length, which [he] supposed to be most
> likely nothing other than the *labia minora,* which he could not
> however say with certainty.

De Blainville was disappointed. Saartjie's genitals appeared to be entirely ordinary in both appearance and dimension. Frustrated, he decided to ignore the empirical evidence, and lean his conclusions on
travel accounts:

> [A]s to whether what was unusual in the bodily organisation
> of this woman derived from a natural disposition of the Hot-
> tentot race, or was the result of a pathological state . . . it was
> easy to show, on the basis of reports by the best
> travellers . . . the extraordinary enlargement of the buttocks
> and the prolongation of the *labia minora* [which he had not
> seen in Saartjie] also being natural to it, but only achieving
> their greatest development with age, and more particularly
> with pregnancy.

With a final misogynist flourish, de Blainville concluded that
Saartjie's labia minora would have been more visibly pronounced
had she been older, or pregnant.

Cuvier's method was different. He approached Saartjie gently, and won her over with a chilling and deceptive caddish courtesy. "She was," he said like a gallant, "good enough to undress and allow herself to be painted from the nude."

Resolute in her strategic placement of the carefully negotiated handkerchief, Saartjie posed before the scientists and artists at the museum in unmistakable imitation of Botticelli's Venus rising from the sea, her auburn tresses cupped to conceal her vagina behind her hand. After her three days of life modeling, Berré, Huet, and de Wailly had produced a series of paintings that became Saartjie's most enduring and famous portraits. (In 2002, de Wailly's portrait was chosen by the South African government as Saartjie's official national image.) These paintings were intended to join the flora and fauna collections in the library of the Museum of Natural History, as well as to illustrate the published works of the scientists.

Huet depicted Saartjie in stark, anatomically defined profile, emphasizing her buttocks. In terms of the Platonic assertion that there are two ideal Venuses, one celestial, the other vulgar, Huet's image is a realist *Venus Naturalis*. Far from outlandish or unfamiliar to the Western eye, the evolving conventions of the female nude in European art are superimposed on this image of Saartjie.

De Wailly's portrait positions Saartjie in an undulating landscape dotted with palm trees, signs of the exotic notwithstanding the fact that they occurred nowhere in the Cape Colony. In this classically proportioned frontal nude, the alien flora frame Saartjie in a nostalgic reference to her lost home. De Wailly's gentle portrait of her face suggests he felt some compassion towards Saartjie's displacement. Her troubled eyes gaze back at the viewer with an expression of deep sadness. Her eyes draw attention away from her nudity, and, as with all the best portraiture, create in the viewer the illusion of being directly looked at, and challenged. De Wailly's Saartjie stands in the classic antique pose of the Cnidian Venus, so beloved of Renaissance sculptors; this figure would reappear later in the nineteenth century in the orientalist *grandes odalisques* of Ingres and Renoir.

Berré's painting shows Saartjie from five perspectives, and his por-

trait of her face is the most romantic. Her softly curled hair frames a
smiling face, lips slightly parted to reveal a seductive flash of teeth.
This image was produced in two versions: one with Saartjie naked,
one in a luridly pink tasseled mini-apron. Berré's engraving was used
to illustrate de Blainville's lecture on Saartjie when it was first published in a scientific journal in 1816. In this image, de Blainville's invented elongated labia minora hang suspended from Saartjie's
neatly trimmed pubic *mons Veneris,* and coyly tucked between her
thighs, a visual lie to support de Blainville's specious argument. Having never got behind the handkerchief, de Blainville simply invented
fabulous, swinging pudenda in his feverish imagination. Outside the
frame of the picture, beneath Saartjie's feet, lies a detailed and
pornographically explicit cartouche of a vagina detached from the
body. Its labia are depicted as flying wings, taking off beneath a soft
pile of pubic hair, the whole framing the smooth dark cherry of an
engorged clitoris, underneath which the white aperture of the
vagina glints in a suggestive smile.

Significantly, it is only between the elite covers of this scholarly
journal that Berré's image appears in this explicit form of scientific
erotica. Elsewhere, the highly ornate, brightly painted girdle of
Venus has been added, tied around Saartjie's waist, a suggestive
fringe concealing her *mons Veneris.* Thus exactly the same image was
used to represent the opposing views of the secret of the "Hottentot
apron": as natural pathology of the body, and as cultural fashion accessory.

Cuvier, Saartjie noticed, went out of his way to disarm her. As
many models before her discovered, life modeling was boring and
uncomfortable. She shifted on her plinth, longing to stretch the stiff
arm that held her handkerchief to her concealed genitals. Cuvier,
however, tried to signal his difference from the other men present.
Apparently ignoring the anomalous situation, he spoke to Saartjie
with chivalry, as if at a soirée where gentlemanliness required him to
be solicitous of her needs. He offered her refreshments, asked for
her compliance with his studies with quiet courtesy, and made little
jokes that, in spite of herself, made Saartjie burst into laughter. All of

this disarming behavior concealed Cuvier's true intentions; in her presence constantly for three days, he had conceived a passion for Saartjie that would not be satisfied until he possessed her completely.

Cuvier's fascination with Saartjie became a morbid, deeply eroticized obsession. His objectifying scientific gaze was indistinguishable from sexual curiosity, the compulsions of desire, and the intense erotic charge of physical difference she awakened in him. Through this most famous Venus the scientist enacted his rage against all women, whom he regarded as excessive, fecund, and untrustworthy creatures whose natural reproductive abilities exceeded all his strenuous godlike attempts to name, order, classify, and thus subdue, the world around him.

On March 18, only a few days after Saartjie had gone to the museum to be drawn, de Blainville delivered the first draft of his paper, entitled "On a Woman of the Hottentot Race," to the Société Philomathique de Paris. Two days later, Napoleon reentered Paris. Nine days after his return, on March 29, France once again abolished the slave trade.

Chapter 10

THE DEATH OF VENUS

§AARTJIE NEVER FULLY recovered from her severe illness of the winter of 1814. While the iconic status of *la Vénus Hottentote* strengthened, the real Saartjie languished and weakened, from overwork, alcohol, and loss of hope. Réaux no longer pressured her to perform regularly. Increasingly reclusive, Saartjie withdrew into a rapid, painful decline. She had played out her last season on the Parisian stage and her fame was now the reflected light of a dying star.

Without the daily routine of her show, Saartjie became listless. Increasingly, she went out only after dark, to entertain the beau monde at private audiences, or to wander in the anonymity of the night in the nearby Palais Royal gardens. Her health was failing, and she needed drink, her only reassurance and constant companion in her disintegrating world. Into this unstructured void, Réaux poured more and more of the spirits she demanded.

Brandy—*eau-de-vie*—stimulated Saartjie's enervated body and spirit, suffusing her with warmth. *Eau-de-vie*, the water of life, was also the agent that the scientists at the Museum of Natural History used as embalming fluid for their specimens. Formaldehyde, which was to provide scientists with more stable formalin solutions, was not introduced until 1893. Until then, potentially volatile spirits of alcohol were employed as both fixative and preservative for all human and animal tissue. Cuvier had noted Saartjie's preference for *eau-de-vie* when he met her for the second time.

It has been claimed that Saartjie became a prostitute towards the end of her life. While there is no documented evidence for this, it is possible that Réaux pimped her to selected clients. Saartjie was aware that Réaux watched her closely, as if weighing the meat on her bones, measuring her failing resistance to illness. The episode at the Jardin du Roi (now restored to its republican name, the Jardin des Plantes) made it apparent to Réaux that Saartjie was now probably worth more to him dead than alive.

The professorial board had discreetly indicated their interest to Réaux following Saartjie's appearance before them at the Jardin des Plantes. Should she happen to die, they would be pleased to pay a sum of money on the delivery of her corpse for the purposes of anatomical dissection. Such highly secretive arrangements had long been common practice between keepers of theatrical wonders, surgeons, and anatomists. Réaux had done well out of Saartjie's live exhibition, and now he could capitalize on her death.

Saartjie slipped away, the last months of her life lost to a succession of illnesses. Repeated attacks of the flu and bronchitis, lack of proper medical care, and excessive drinking left her vulnerable to respiratory disease.

The winter of 1815 was bitterly cold and harsh. Saartjie died at 7 Cour des Fontaines during the night of Friday, December 29. Réaux did not call a priest. That is all we know.

IN THE ICY DAWN OF SATURDAY the thirtieth, Réaux left 7 Cour des Fontaines, walking briskly towards the Jardin des Plantes. City law required that deaths be declared immediately to the municipal authorities at the Mairie. Réaux, however, was walking resolutely in the wrong direction, to the homes of Saint-Hilaire and Cuvier, who lived on the grounds of the Museum of Natural History.

Awoken by Réaux, with whom he had a hurried conference, Saint-Hilaire immediately wrote two urgent letters. First, to the mayor, whom he notified of Saartjie's death. Réaux, he slyly informed the mayor, was on his way to register her death officially with the municipality. In the meantime, however, Saint-Hilaire was writing to give the mayor advance warning of his intention to remove Saartjie's body to the museum's anatomy laboratories "in the interests of the progress of human knowledge."

Next, Saint-Hilaire wrote to the Comte Anglès, minister of state and prefect of police, requesting permission to take Saartjie's body to the museum:

> Dear Sir
>
> A woman of the Kaffir country shown by Mr. Réaux under the name of the HOTTENTOT VENUS has just died in the Cour des Fontaines. This opportunity to acquire new information on this singular race of the human species leads us to ask you for permission for the body of this woman to be transported to the Anatomy Laboratory of the Natural History Museum.
>
> My colleague Mr. Cuvier, who is responsible at the museum for the teaching of comparative anatomy begs me to assure you that he will see that all measures required by decency and appropriate to the circumstances should be rigorously implemented in the interest of public order.

The Museum of Natural History was not officially permitted to receive bodies for educational or scientific purposes. A decree of 1813 authorized legal dissection only at the medical faculty of the University of Paris and the Petie Hospital. According to this directive, remains should be taken to the Clamart cemetery for proper burial after dissection. The Museum of Natural History therefore had no legal right to dissect Saartjie. Saint-Hilaire was asking the chief of police to bend the law. He obliged, authorizing "Sarjee's" corpse to be moved to the museum, subject to the conditions that Saint-Hilaire would be:

> (1) taking the necessary measures to preserve decency and
> (2) co-ordinating for these purposes with the Commissioner of Police for the Palais Royal district, who will draw up an official minute recording the handover of the body.

Less than twenty-four hours after her death, without the solemnizing of any rites, Saartjie's body was delivered to the Museum of Natural History. Two documents were found carefully folded among her personal possessions: a copy of her contract with Dunlop, and her 1811 baptismal certificate. Réaux handed over the documents with her corpse. Among her remaining effects: a crumpled handkerchief.

NIGHT CLOSED AROUND the firmly secured shutters of the anatomical laboratory in the Jardin des Plantes. Inside, the dissection of the Hottentot Venus was under way. At the center of proceedings, steely-hearted Cuvier, with his knives and saws, concentrated deeply; cutting into Saartjie, naked, on her back on his sepulchral anatomy bench. Her tortoiseshell pendant had been removed from her neck. Cuvier had finally got what he desired—Saartjie, horizontal, unresisting, under his knife.

Cuvier's assistants bustled around the laboratory, helping at the bench, clearing blood, and laying out perishable organs. Others checked the setting of the plaster body casts taken directly from Saartjie's cadaver. Lard and plant oil were stirred into the viscous, boiling solution of Chinese wax to keep it the right consistency for taking molds of her soft-tissued organs. Large glass bell jars were set out on a workbench alongside flagons of distilled alcohol and potassium hydroxide, as if in preparation for the mixing of a cocktail for a giant. The bell jars and *eau-de-vie* were for the fluid preservation of Saartjie's brain and genitals; the potassium hydroxide (caustic potash) for the boiling of her bones.

By Monday morning, Cuvier and his team had completed the critical preliminary work on Saartjie's corpse. Plaster casts had been taken of her body. Once the whole figure was integrated, "sculptors and artists finished the lines to the mould, polished the model surface with oil of turpentine, and then skin, vessels and body surface were painted on; the whole covered in a coat of clear varnish."

Cuvier performed a postmortem examination and full dissection, concluding with the removal of Saartjie's brain. He sliced Saartjie's flesh around her hairline, peeled back her face, sawed through her cranium, removed her brain, embalming it in a glass bell jar of *eau-de-vie*. Thirty-eight years later Pierre Gratiolet would study this specimen. In 1864 Professor Thomas Henry Huxley would cite Gratiolet's work on Saartjie's brain in a lecture that argued in favor of "Negro" emancipation from slavery in America.

Cuvier, however, was more interested in Saartjie's labia, clitoris, vagina, and buttocks than her brain. Her genital organs were modeled in wax and the originals stoppered in a bell jar awash with *eau-de-vie*. Cuvier thus secured himself both dry and wet preparations of his Venus's genitalia.

The long labor of casting and dissection completed, Cuvier ordered the cleaning of the bloody laboratory, and supervised the disarticulation of Saartjie's skeleton, taking immense care with its preservation.

An "entire skeleton" is a thing "infinitely precious," Cuvier once said, referring to the difficulty of obtaining them for comparative anatomy. Cuvier described his method in the instructions he issued to his more adventurous colleagues in the anthropological society regarding how to collect skeletons. If voyagers saw or took part in "battles with savages," they were to make every effort to find "the places where the dead are deposited" and obtain skeletons "in any manner whatever." Each skeleton, Cuvier explained,

> should be boiled in caustic potash for several hours to remove the flesh, after which the bones were to be put in a bag, labelled and sent back to Europe where they might be reassembled. It would also be desirable to bring back some skulls with the flesh still intact. . . . [T]he sailors might oppose all this as barbarous, but the leaders must remember that a scientific expedition should be governed only by reason.

What luck for timid, travel-wary Cuvier. No need to do battle with savages, seek out umbrageous burial grounds, strip human bones in boiling cauldrons, or fear offending the sensibilities of sailors. His

Hottentot Venus had come directly to his doorstep in the heart of Paris.

NEWS OF SAARTJIE'S DEATH made the Saturday papers. The *Journal Général de France* claimed that the Hottentot Venus had died that morning, "after a short illness of three days." *"La Vénus hottentote est morte,"* announced another. On Monday the first of January, *Annales Politiques, Morales et Littéraires* informed its readers of Saartjie's dissection. This potpourri of prejudice, racial condescension, and ethnographic myth typifies the many articles published immediately following Saartjie's death:

> Just now, in one of the rooms of the Museum of Natural History, they are busy taking a mould of the Hottentot Venus, who died on the day before yesterday of an ataxic fever [a type of syphilis of the nervous system]. . . . Her general plumpness and her enormous protuberances are not diminished, and her extremely frizzy hair has not at all lengthened, as is ordinarily the case in Negroes during illness or after death. The dissection of this woman will provide M. Cuvier with an extremely curious chapter for his account of the varieties of the human species. *The Hottentot Venus* provided the subject for plays and caricatures; she will now be the subject only of the naturalist's scalpel, and afterwards certain material parts of this divinity will have no other Olympus than a glass jar.

So famed were Saartjie's "enormous protuberances" that they needed no specification.

Obituaries followed, propagating a rumor that Saartjie had died of smallpox. The *Journal Général de France* berated Réaux for his "mindless obstinacy" in not following advice "to have his monster vaccinated." *Mercure de France* huffed, "What proves that the Hottentot Venus wasn't really acclimatized is that she died of the *smallpox.* Our European Venuses would never have died of such a bagatelle."

Cuvier's conclusion on the cause of Saartjie's death was that she died of an unspecified "eruptive and inflammatory disease" (*"maladie inflammatoire et éruptive"*). Extrapolating from this, it has been suggested that she died from one or a combination of the following: pneumonia, pleurisy, smallpox, or syphilis. Speedily fatal chest diseases are certainly consistent with what we know of Saartjie's battle against influenza. However, the claim that she was carried off by the "French pox," or syphilis, reflected popular prejudice, not medical fact. The notion of Saartjie as lonely, venal Venus decomposing from the pox would within a few decades make her the preeminent icon of atavistic sexuality in nineteenth-century European art and literature, from Zola to Baudelaire, Manet to Picasso. These legends took root in the immediate wake of her untimely death.

Assertions that Saartjie died of smallpox ignored the well-known dangers of handling a pustulant cadaver, and overlooked the fact that the body casts show none of the chancrous disfigurations specifically associated with death from this disease. Saartjie's death masks heartbreakingly show that her face was painfully swollen and her eyes puffy as she died. These symptoms do not prove smallpox, and are equally consistent with alcoholism and fatal pneumonia. The unproven possibility remains that she died from syphilis of the nervous system, known medically as locomotor ataxia or *tabes dorsalis*.

Cuvier's opinion was that it was probably *eau-de-vie* that finally carried off Saartjie. "Her death might even be attributed to the excessive drinking in which she indulged during her last illness," he wrote, deploying the standard qualifier typical of postmortem reports. In other words, her last illness was not inevitably life threatening, but her alcoholism prevented her body from fighting this final pathogenic onslaught.

Oddly enough, Saartjie's death coincided with the repatriation to Italy of the famous Roman statue known as the Medici Venus. "Nothing but loss for ideal beauty" was the laconic remark of the diarist of *L'Ambigu*. "[T]he artists no longer have their *Venus alba,* but it is the naturalists who have got hold of the *Venus nigra.*" Plundered from the Palazzo Uffizi by Napoleon, the celebrated Hellenistic statue had arrived in Paris in 1802. At the end of December 1815, it was crated up and sent back to Florence. The English press was much taken with this coincidence. Fleet Street, predictably, went for the bottom line:

The Venus of Medicis *scarcely has flown,*
When Paris, alas! Your next Venus is gone;
And no end to your losses you find:
Well may you in sackcloth and ashes deplore;
For the former *fair form had no equal* before,
And the latter no equal behind.

From the day after she died, Saartjie's unburied relics remained close to Cuvier until his own death and dissection. His apartments at the Museum of Natural History opened directly onto the upper floor of his famous Cabinet d'Anatomie Comparée, by way of an interconnecting mirrored door. The Lancastrian comparative anatomist Richard Owen (who coined the term *dinosauria* to describe giant extinct reptiles) visited the museum in 1822, and revealed that the bell jars containing Saartjie's brain and genitals were kept directly outside the door to Cuvier's private apartments. These specimens, Owen stated, were preserved in "bottles of a rude shape," without feet, and made from "common greenish glass." The preparations were "dropped in without any mode of suspension" and were "dimly visible through the dirty spirit."

Saartjie's skeleton was also in Cuvier's upper gallery, among 1,599 others, forty-one of which were human, "of the various races." These included three Egyptian mummies, the so-called Assassin of Kleber, an Italian with an extra lumbar vertebra, eleven other "Negroes or Hottentots," and Bébé, the deposed Polish King Stanislas's dwarf.

A whole apartment twenty feet square was dedicated to two thousand skulls kept behind glass, including "a great number of European, Tartar, Chinese, Maori, Negro and Hottentot skulls, and also examples of the South American races." One chamber housed the bones of the hand and foot, while another contained larger disconnected dry bones: femurs, hip bones, back bones, shoulder bones.

Here it was that Saartjie's unburied remains were kept under lock and key, secured behind glass, protected "from the hands of any but privileged visitors." It was from here, and from collections like this one, that the pseudosciences of ethnography and scientific racism were invented in order to propose theories about human racial difference.

After his dinner, Cuvier would take his notebook into his gallery of natural classification, where he worked deep into the night, trying to penetrate the recesses of nature, looking for the patterns that he believed would reveal the deepest mysteries of creation, and of African female sexuality. Cuvier's brother Frédéric described him privately as "master of the charnel house." The Cabinet D'Anatomie was not, at this stage, open to the public. Saartjie's body, in life a popular spectacle, became in death a rarefied relic, locked away, viewable, touchable, only by the connoisseur—the captive property of science.

Linnaeus and Buffon had described the exteriors of living and fossil forms; Cuvier studied the interiors. For previous zoologists, classification was based on external resemblances, but Cuvier argued that zoology was worthless without comparative anatomy. Anti-Lamarckian, opposed to the notion of a natural hierarchy (*scala naturae*), and antievolutionist, Cuvier was the first to define the principle that the classification of animals should be based on comparative anatomy. The founder of paleontology, he used the anatomy of recent animals to aid in the reconstruction of extinct fossil forms.

At the beginning of 1832, Baron Cuvier was made a peer of France and, shortly before his unexpected death four months later, was appointed minister of the interior. Crowds pressed the processional route to Père Lachaise cemetery, where he was honored with an extravagant state funeral. No such honor or courtesy had been extended to Saartjie. Her nemesis had left the charnel house, but her body parts remained immured in the Museum of Natural History.

Cuvier's body was also dissected following his own precise instructions. His brain was found to be "unusually heavy" (1,860 grams) and "exceptional in the bulging configuration of the lobes." In a 1908 study that ranked the capacities of 115 "men of note" by brain weight, Turgenev's came first, Cuvier's third. Women's brains were excluded from the study.

One and a half centuries later, the bell jar containing Saartjie's preserved genitals was rediscovered stored alongside the brains of illustrious nineteenth-century scientists, "all white and all male," including Cuvier's. The paleontologist Stephen Jay Gould, in search of the preserved brain of the famous scientist Paul Broca, looked up and saw, amid the accumulated gray matter of the male intelligentsia, three jars labeled "une négresse," "une péruvienne," and "la Vénus Hottentote."

Saartjie's bottom became one of the most famous physical objects of the nineteenth century; yet unlike her brain, it was not preserved as physical matter, but as legend, popular myth, caricature, and racist stereotype. Drawing on Saartjie's legacy, Charles Darwin and Henry Havelock Ellis preoccupied themselves with the racial and sexual signification of black buttocks. Darwin typified the generally held European view that the bottoms of so-called Hottentot women provided a "somewhat comic sign of the primitive, grotesque nature of black female sexuality." French and British pornographers shared this fascination, and profited from its exploitation.

From successive dissection and analysis of Saartjie's remains, Western European science invented improbable and degrading theories about the bodies of Khoisan women. These disciplines attempted to dignify and justify their prejudice by claiming that big bottoms were not simply natural physiology, but a medical condition that they categorized as "steatopygia." For all its vaunted rational objectivity, there was evidently an underlying agenda: the pursuit of fantasies about primitive and unconstrained, thus "uncivilized," female sexual appetites, which both fascinated and appalled masculine intellectual elites.

In 1850 Charles Darwin's cousin Francis Galton, who later coined the term *eugenics,* visited what is today Namibia, where he was fascinated to meet a "Venus among Hottentots," endowed with "that gift of bounteous nature to this favoured race, which no mantua-maker, with all her crinoline and stuffing, can do otherwise than humbly imitate." Galton "boldly pulled out" his measuring tape and sextant to evaluate the privy parts and nether regions of a woman he likened to the legendary Saartjie. Galton's bottom-measuring "experiment" provided a telling remark about the contemporary fashion for the artificially built-up bottom. Later in the nineteenth century, the streets of London, the boulevards of Paris, and the thoroughfares of Cape Town through which she had walked were teeming with women got up in synthetically constructed fashion steatopygia, vaunted as the height of civilized European style. What the English mincingly referred to as the tournure dress improver, or bustle, the French called simply *le faux-cul*—the false bum.

In Galton's time, this combination of whalebone, crinoline, and stuffing was the only option available for simulating a large bottom. Galton could hardly have anticipated that two centuries later surgeons would be redrawing the outlines of the female gluteus maximus with scalpels and silicone implants. At the beginning of the twenty-first century, buttock augmentation surgery became the fastest-growing cosmetic procedure in America and Europe. In Britain, the demand for the "plump rump" increased tenfold, while across the Atlantic, there was a fivefold increase. Patients report the pain to be excruciating, but are delighted and amazed by the end results.

Could the great men of nineteenth-century science who had so much to say on the subject of Saartjie's bottom—Cuvier, de Blainville, Darwin, and Havelock Ellis—have imagined that generations later their professional descendants would be performing surgery on women with gluteal deficiencies in order to re-create them in the image of the Hottentot Venus?

How Saartjie would have laughed.

Chapter 11
LAYING DOWN THE BONES

I̱T TOOK SAARTJIE THREE MONTHS to get to Europe, and almost two centuries to get back home to South Africa.

At an unknown date between 1822 and the 1850s, the keepers of the National Museum of Natural History placed Saartjie's skeleton, body cast, brain, and genitals on public display; and there they remained until the 1970s, when the bottled specimens, skeleton, and body cast were removed from open exhibition. Then, in 1982, as previously mentioned, Saartjie's brain and genitalia were accidentally rediscovered by Stephen Jay Gould in the museum's storerooms.

Fittingly, the end of apartheid in South Africa was the crucial turning point in Saartjie's afterlife. In 1994, the year the African National Congress achieved the country's transition to nonracial democracy, then-president Nelson Mandela raised the matter of Saartjie directly with the French president, François Mitterrand, during his first state visit to South Africa. In formally declaring right of possession to Saartjie's remains, Mandela declared the new state's commitment to honoring her as a heroic ancestor, and made the first international act of reclaiming cultural property on behalf of the people of free South Africa.

In 1995 Ben Ngubane, minister of the Department of Arts, Culture, Science and Technology (DACST), announced the government's intention to have Saartjie's remains returned for proper and dignified burial in the land of her birth:

[S]he was a known-in-life person and a symbol of an era of oppression and colonialism, her remains should be repatriated
to South Africa, without any imputation that either England
or France, the French Government, the French people or
scholars are to be blamed for the parlous treatment which she
received in Europe between 1810 and 1815.

South African paleoanthropologist professor Phillip Tobias, a lifelong
campaigner for the repatriation of Saartjie's remains, was appointed
to lead the negotiations with the French authorities. His chief negotiating partner was the museologist professor Henry de Lumley,
then director of the Museum of Mankind and the Museum of Natural History in Paris, and therefore the official custodian of Saartjie's
remains.

Saartjie quickly became a potent symbol for political and cultural
restitution. The National Khoisan Consultative Conference, led by
Cecil Le Fleur, who lobbied for international recognition of the
Khoisan as indigenous first peoples, also pressed the French government to send back Saartjie's relics. In their view, Saartjie represented
the suffering of all Khoisan people. Women's rights activists, poets,
artists, academics, and politicians raised their voices on Saartjie's behalf. In August 1998, the United Nations Working Group on Indigenous Populations accorded first-nation status to the Khoisan,
strengthening the call for Saartjie's return.

From the outset of the protracted negotiations, South Africa
made it clear to France that it regarded Saartjie's case as unique, not
as the forerunner of similar requests for the repatriation of the thousands of skulls, skeletons, and cultural objects in museums in Europe, North America, and Australasia, which had been removed
during colonial times, mostly without the informed consent of their
rightful owners. Saartjie was a special case, who had become, in
Phillip Tobias's words, an "international symbol of colonial and imperial excesses." At the national level, another argument supported
the claim; there were many Baartmans living in South Africa who
might share Saartjie's lineage.

The French museums proved initially resistant, anxious that Saartjie's release would create a flood of further requests from post-colonial nation-states for the return of artifacts plundered by imperial adventurers, stripping Western museums. At first de Lumley resisted, arrogantly claiming that Saartjie's relics would be safer "cherished in the home of liberty, fraternity and equality, than in South Africa." Brigitte Mabandla, deputy minister of DACST, challenged this intransigence:

The end of colonialism is tied to the return of Africa's cultural heritage: Europe doesn't understand the passion of many colonized peoples to right the wrongs of the past. Scholars argue that two hundred year old remains should be classified as ordinary artifacts, and tools for research, and that there is no need to attach emotions to them. This is a fallacy. Europe is littered with ancient heritage, and there is a lot of passion associated with heritage by the Europeans themselves. Humankind remains attached to what is valuable and cultural. Saartjie Baartman's remains are very meaningful to a large majority of South Africans.

Classified as French national patrimony, Saartjie's remains could not leave the country permanently unless allowed by a specific change in the law. By October 2000, dialogue had reached an impasse. In November, Ben Ngubane interceded, supported by President Thabo Mbeki, and broke the deadlock. The highly publicized return of El Negro from Spain to Botswana augmented the legitimacy of South Africa's request for Saartjie.

Saartjie also had political allies in France who ardently supported South Africa's claim for her return—in particular, the French research minister Roger-Gerard Schwartzenberg and senator Nicolas About, who set about framing legislation to permit the repatriation of her remains. Speaking in the French Senate, Schwartzenberg said that Saartjie's return would mark Europe's emergence "from the long night of slavery, colonialism, and racism," also observing that the law would "restore full dignity to Saartjie Baartman, who was humiliated as a woman and exploited as an African." Nicolas About made a passionate address: "This young woman was treated as if she was something monstrous. But where in this affair is the true monstrosity?" He also read out "I've come to take you home—a tribute to Sarah Baartman" by the South African poet Diana Ferrus, who is of Khoisan descent. Ferrus's poem was highly influential in persuading the Senate to support the bill, giving Saartjie a human face and personalizing her plight. On January 29, 2002, the Senate voted to release Saartjie's remains. The legislation went to the National Assembly for approval, and on February 21, 2002, it voted unanimously for Saartjie's return to South Africa.

On April 29 the French government formally handed over Saartjie's remains in a ceremony held at the South African embassy in Paris. Thuthukile Skweyiya, South African ambassador to France, announced, "Saartjie Baartman is beginning her final journey home, to a free, democratic, non-sexist and non-racist South Africa. She is a symbol of our national need to confront our past and restore dignity to all our people."

Specialized packagers of human remains had carefully arranged Saartjie's diminutive skeleton, pearl white and luminous, in a foam-lined box. The two glass bell jars and the full-body plaster cast were also crated and returned.

South African Airways flight number 275 flew through the night of May 2, 2002, from Paris to Johannesburg, bearing its historic cargo. Just before the plane landed, the captain announced that it was carrying a very special passenger. This time, Saartjie had not traveled in secret.

Saartjie's remains touched South African soil on the bright highveld morning of May 3, 2002. After 187 years, she was home. South Africa greeted her with a rapturous reception, and her repatriation hit the headlines in the national and global media. From Johannesburg, Saartjie's relics were flown to Cape Town International Airport, where once again crowds gathered to welcome her. Shrouded by the new South African flag, her casket was lowered onto the runway to the accompaniment of a small band of Cape musicians, one of whom played a *ramkie*. Children pressed their faces against the windows of the arrivals terminal. A military band accompanied the official welcoming ceremony, including, elegiacally, a smartly uniformed young drummer.

After much public debate, Hankey, a small rural town near the banks of the Gamtoos River, was chosen as Saartjie's final resting place. The rocky mount (*koppie*) chosen for Saartjie's grave is called Vergaderingskop, meaning "meeting hill." Vergaderingskop overlooks the emerald green and incarnadine earth of the Gamtoos River Valley, encircled by indigo mountains and sheltered by a sky that, in the words of the Langston Hughes poem read by President Mbeki at Saartjie's burial, turns "all golden in the sunset." The funeral date was set for August 9, Women's Day in South Africa and international Indigenous Peoples' Day. On Sunday August 4, 2002, a Khoisan cleansing ritual and dressing ceremony, combining tradition and invention, took place at the Cape Town civic theater, to prepare Saartjie for burial.

Saartjie's return became a rallying point for the descendants of Khoisan people in search of their ancestral identity. The funeral preparations caused some discord among indigenous interest groups, who felt that they had been excluded from the consultation process, and that politicians had hijacked Saartjie's homecoming. Some families claimed to be Saartjie's direct descendants. Khoisan historian Nealroy Swarts questioned the reliability of these assertions, but welcomed the debate: "It is good to know that people are starting to make claims of their heritage. That is something we must be proud of. This is our grandmother. This is the nation's grandmother."

Baartman is a very common South African surname; there are Baartmans among all races and religions. While there is currently no firm evidence confirming Saartjie's immediate family descendants, academics continue to research her lineage, and perhaps may solve the question. Saartjie became a powerful symbol of integration and inclusion for all South Africa's formerly divided racial groups.

Saartjie also became a representative figure in South Africa's struggle for gender equality. In parliament, South African women MPs condemned her exploitation and welcomed the restoration of her dignity. She was honored nationwide by women's rights activists at rallies and demonstrations. A shelter for women and children subjected to domestic and sexual violence is named after her.

Addressing so many live issues in South Africa, Saartjie became a living ancestor. Nations, like individuals, need myths and icons to salve and heal the psychological and physical injuries inflicted by oppressive systems and internalized over centuries of marginalization. Saartjie's homecoming was a tangible act to right a historical wrong. The public rituals of mourning and acknowledgment of the injustice she endured provided a means of addressing buried suffering.

About two and a half thousand people attended Saartjie's state funeral on August 9, 2002. The day was dazzling and fiercely hot. Beyond the ministerial enclosures, the throng of celebrants sheltered themselves as best they could from the pitiless sun. It was a day of music, dance, poetry, theater, praise singing, and speeches. Reporting from the funeral on live national television, SABC News anchor Redi Direko summarized the atmosphere:

> Rarely has one figure meant so much to an entire country. In the burial of Saartjie Baartman we have so many issues coming together; the issues of culture, the issues of identity, the issues of cultural reparation after all these years.

Young girls cavorted, perhaps somewhat incongruously, in scanty bushbuck bikinis. A syncopated diaspora of women of all ages and ethnicities danced together in fine African beadwork, rustling Indian saris, and *doeks* (head scarves). The euphonious sounds of friction bows, *gouras,* and Saartjie's beloved *ramkie* could be heard all day. Diana Ferrus read aloud her now-famous poem, and proclaimed Saartjie South Africa's great mother and ancestor. Women's leaders, represented by the South African Commission on Gender Equality, said that the greatest tribute South Africa could pay Saartjie was to work for the liberation of women from sexual slavery, violence, abuse, poverty, and disease.

Speakers at the funeral emphasized that Saartjie's homecoming empowered Africans to reclaim personal dignity, and helped the continent to overcome its marginalization. Nealroy Swarts reminded the mourners that European colonization had decimated Khoisan culture and society. Ben Ngubane commemorated Saartjie's ancestors and descendants: "[T]hey were all victims of a vicious system, a system that could declare a people, a land, a culture, to be subservient to a distant monarch somewhere in Europe." Brigitte Mabandla described how, when visiting schools, she found that every child knew about Saartjie. Her life, the deputy minister said, should be taught as part of the school history curriculum, as an example for the rejection of racist historical iconography. Saartjie's story, Mabandla concluded, offers "an education for the public in our own past."

The remembrance and revision of racist history and science were the central themes of President Thabo Mbeki's speech. Mbeki illustrated how Saartjie was exploited by leading European scientists to prove their xenophobic notions of white superiority. He discussed the racist observations to be found in the work of leading philosophers of the Enlightenment, such as Voltaire, Montesquieu, and Diderot. Juxtaposing notions of European civilization with historical assumptions about African barbarism, he reversed this logic to demonstrate the barbarism of ostensibly civilized European culture. Mbeki said that by supporting Saartjie's rightful repatriation, the French had finally lived up to the noble objectives of liberty, equality, and fraternity. Apartheid, he reminded his listeners, was also "based on the criminal notion that some had been called upon to enlighten the hordes of barbarians, as Sarah Bartmann was enlightened and tamed."

The president congratulated all women on National Women's Day, marking South Africa's responsibility to move speedily towards the creation of a nonsexist society. Women, Mbeki said, bore the brunt of oppression and exploitation under colonial and apartheid

domination: "They, more than the African male, were presented as
the very representation of what was savage and barbaric about all our
people." Even today, he reminded his audience, women in South
Africa continue to carry the burden of poverty, unacceptable violence, and abuse.

Mbeki stressed that the nation identified with the burden of
Saartjie's pain and intolerable misery: "When we turn away from this
grave of a simple African woman, a particle of each one of us will stay
with the remains of Sarah Bartmann." Intended as respectful, this
reference to Saartjie as a simple African woman struck an odd, pa-
tronizing note. Mbeki's speech clearly accounted for the ways in
which Saartjie was sexually and racially subjugated as an object of
pornographic representation, but made no comment on the exploitation of her physical, economic labor, either as a domestic servant or a "carnal curiosity."

Mbeki's speech at Saartjie's funeral focused on the role of medical
history in the sexual ideology of colonial and apartheid racism. His
critical analysis of the nineteenth-century European scientists and
philosophers who abused the body of Saartjie Baartman was accurate, but the manner in which he yoked this history to an attempt to
justify his own public health policies was not. As is well known, President Mbeki controversially denies the causal link between the HIV
virus and AIDS, a position that has come to be known as a policy of
denialism. Mbeki has also supported claims that anti-retroviral drugs
are ineffective and lethally toxic, in the face of massive scientific evidence to the contrary, and in contradiction of the experience of people living with HIV who have access to ARV treatment. In July 2000,
at the 13th International AIDS Conference in Durban, South Africa,
five thousand researchers and scientists from around the world issued the "Durban Declaration" to challenge Mbeki, insisting that
HIV causes AIDS, a statement that his press secretary declared as fit
only for the "dustbin." Mbeki's reluctance to make AIDS drugs available, and his perceived support for the right wing American AIDS
"dissidents," have led critics from within South Africa and the rest of
the world to charge Mbeki with "irresponsibility bordering on crimi-

nality." In 2000, Mbeki appointed two controversial American AIDS dissidents, who defy mainstream opinion that AIDS is caused by the HIV virus, to a presidential advisory board on the epidemic. Nelson Mandela has publicly rebuked Mbeki for his stance on AIDS in South Africa. Thus the focus of this speech at Saartjie's funeral was significant. When Thabo Mbeki talks about European science and its relation to Africa, the message is clear: he is engaging on the troubled battleground of HIV/AIDS. Allusions to the pandemic haunted his entire funeral address, and this speech is seen as a singular statement on a subject he rarely speaks about in public.

On the hillcrest of Vergaderingskop, the burial ceremony began with the burning of *buchu,* a sweet-smelling medicinal herb, to purify Saartjie's spirit. Khoisan chiefs broke a bow and arrows and scattered them into the grave in traditional observance of the ancestors. As a women's choir sang softly in the background, "You are returning to your fatherland under African skies," Saartjie's coffin, decorated with aloe wreaths, was lowered into the ground.

$\mathcal{S}$AARTJIE DIED IN 1815, and was buried in 2002. Her bones never gathered dust. For two centuries, the Hottentot Venus appeared in European science, art, literature, philosophy, and popular culture, choreographed to the macabre dance of racial and sexual prejudice. European racism made Saartjie a Frankenstein's monster of its own invention. Subdued and dismembered, Saartjie's relics became the haunting agent of her posthumous retribution. Through them, Western imperialism would be called to account for its inhumanity.

Andreas Vesalius, the father of anatomical dissection, believed that "the violation of the body would be the revelation of its truth." Saartjie's disarticulated body became one of Europe's most frequently analyzed specimens. Saartjie's skeleton was rattled, her dead brain dissected, her genital matter fingered by inquisitive European men who believed that her pickled organs held secrets that would reveal the mysteries of the "dark continent" of African female sexuality. From these lifeless and fragile remnants of Saartjie's violated body, scientists manufactured monstrous, crackpot theories proposing biological racial differences among human groups. There was, they argued, more than one species in the genus *Homo;* races could be classified, and ranked in terms of superiority and inferiority. The motivation was obvious: the desire to justify inequalities of power.

De Blainville (in a paper published in 1816) and Cuvier (in one published in 1817) superimposed the template of scientific racism upon Saartjie's remains. Scientists, ethnographers, anthropologists, philosophers, and psychologists followed them. Throughout the nineteenth and twentieth centuries, scientific racism and eugenics exploited Saartjie's dismembered body, using it as the ultimate example to "prove" and propound the belief that races existed, and were biologically different. According to these pseudosciences, Europeans were at the top of the human scale of evolution in the Great Chain of Being, and Africans at the bottom, and the so-called Hottentots and Bushmen of sub-Saharan Africa were the missing link to the animal species. Among the allegedly degenerate and brutally inferior, "Hottentots" were assigned the lowest rank among the admissibly human. British imperialism incorporated this specious science into its ruling ideology in South Africa, and the apartheid regime followed suit.

Although Saartjie lived only a short life, her remains finally outlived the lie of inherent racial difference. The discovery of DNA in the 1950s proved that race is a socially constructed phenomenon with no biological basis, thus consigning scientific racism and eugenics to the dustbin of history. Found in the nucleus of cells, the DNA molecule determines human physical characteristics by providing the set of instructions from which the human body is built. "There are no inferior races: there are no races; there is practically no racial differentiation among humans." In 1950 and 1952, UNESCO's international meetings of scientists declared that race was a social myth, not a biological fact, and that humans belong to the single species *Homo sapiens,* and they recommended dropping the term *race* altogether. Visual differences "in physical structure which distinguish one major group from another give no support to the popular notions of any general 'superiority' or 'inferiority' which are sometimes implied in referring to . . . groups." Scientists told the world that the facts of biology had made racism indefensible and that "[t]he likenesses among men are far greater than their differences."

Science had finally conceded that the visual differences between humans are meaningless. However, the disproving of scientific theories, even when they are publicly and internationally revoked, does not, unfortunately, have the power to reverse and erase the continu-

ing psychic and cultural impact of the legacy of race and racism, as
the example of Saartjie's life demonstrates.

Some expressed hope that Saartjie's burial would drop the final
curtain over her life and lay her spirit to rest. But traumatic memory
is not easily buried. Saartjie's iconic power had already long exceeded her individual story. As journalist and producer Sylvia Vollen-
hoven expressed it on South African television on the day of her
funeral, "Sarah Baartman is no longer Sarah Baartman. She has become a symbol for the women of our country." A symbol of the alien-
ation and degradations of colonization, lost children, exile, the
expropriation of female labor, and the sexual and economic exploitation of black women by men, white and black, Saartjie has
come to represent the pain and suffering of all exploited black
women, and the psychic, cultural, and emotional impact of racism
and its legacy. This was the aspect of her legacy Thabo Mbeki stressed
in his graveside description of Saartjie as "a simple African woman"
who was a passive victim subject entirely to the will of others. However, as with all sanctified women, the archetype of the silenced victim threatens to engulf Saartjie's individualism and humanity. Toni
Morrison has written critically of how, in the conventions of racist
storytelling, a black woman is "[r]endered voiceless, a cipher, a perfect victim." Saartjie suffered, but she endured, and as far as she
could, rebelled. As an orphan, as a woman, as a curious, adventurous
individual, she stepped always on the edge of danger, surviving for as
long as possible in extraordinarily challenging circumstances.

Throughout her life Saartjie had to suffer for her race as well; her
experience prompts an instinctive loyalty to the notion of race and
sexuality as the defining factors in her life, yet this notion leaves her
unfree. It is part of women's historical burden to be made representative, and this is the danger of memorializing her as a passive victim.
As Saartjie experienced throughout her life, being placed on a
pedestal as an object of degradation, veneration, or both, is potentially fatal—and opposable. Sanctification never set a woman's spirit
free. The dangers of not looking for the acts of resistance in Saartjie's
life, however small they may seem now, are greater than those of sen-

timentalizing her story. As long as Saartjie is seen as inescapably constrained by her race and gender, history will still have its foot on her neck.

In life, and after, Saartjie has been a constant preoccupation for men, from soldiers, sailors, doctors, and traders, to scientists, politicians, and philosophers, many of whom were among the most prominent men of their age. Some were progressive, most were not.

More recently, South Africa's first two democratic presidents have taken direct, personal responsibility for Saartjie's legacy. By asking France to return Saartjie, Nelson Mandela announced to the world that South Africa could forgive, but not forget, and that Europe needed to make active reparation for the past. Thabo Mbeki took over the baton and ensured her return; he also brought Saartjie into the front line of the most defining and vexed issues of modern South Africa: the HIV/AIDS crisis, his vision of the African Renaissance, and the legacy of racism.

Saartjie's resting place has not been left in peace. Even on the day of her funeral, rumors sprang up around her grave. A local policeman claimed that the remains buried at Hankey were not hers. According to this canard, the government retained her relics in an undisclosed location because of the risk of extortion: villains might dig them up and hold them to ransom.

In September 2003, the decomposing body of a four-year-old boy was discovered shallowly buried beneath a bush by her grave. In March 2005, vandals removed the memorial nameplate from a rock near her burial place, provoking an angry response from the government. While conspiracy, child murder, and desecration troubled Saartjie's resting place, she was memorialized elsewhere as a preeminent figure in South Africa's ancestral, political, and cultural heritage. In January 2005, the government took delivery of the *Sarah Baartman*, a state-of-the-art offshore environmental protection vessel made in Holland.

Saartjie continues to be a venerated and contested figure in South Africa. The return of her remains has also made her a global icon, as recognized in the annals of British and French history as she is in the townships and schools of South Africa. Founded upon the principle of nonracial democracy, with probably the most progressive democratic constitution in the world, South Africa chose Saartjie as an important ancestor to symbolize the restoration of the dignity and humanity of all its peoples. Controversy and debate will continue to haunt her troubled life and legacy, but it is now possible to say that Saartjie Baartman has truly come home.

ACKNOWLEDGMENTS

FOR ASSISTING ME in discovering the original research on which this biography is based, my thanks to archivists Jackson Zweliyanyikima Vena, Cory Library, Rhodes University, Grahamstown; Erica Le Roux, Cape Town Archives Repository; and Mike Bevan, National Maritime Museum, Greenwich. I am grateful to Geoffrey Robinson, Parish Clerk and Head Verger, for sparing the time to give me advice and instruction on the Parish Registers in Manchester Cathedral Archives. Other important sources included the collections of the Museum Africa, Johannesburg; National Library of South Africa, Cape Town; the Archives of the Royal Society London; the Royal College of Surgeons of England Library and Archive; the Wellcome Library for the History and Understanding of Medicine; the British Library; the London Library; the Collingdale Newspaper Library; Lambeth Palace Library; The National Archives of the United Kingdom, Kew, Surrey; the Norfolk Record Office, Norwich; la Bibliothèque nationale de France and le Musée national d'histoire naturelle, Paris.

Thanks to the Ferreira sisters and the women at the Purple Orange Café in Hankey.

I am very grateful to friends and colleagues for additional research, translations, and sharing their expertise: Jean Blanckenberg, Heather Ewing, Margaret Reynolds, Daffyd Roberts, and Robert Symonds.

Many thanks to Midi Achmat, Dhianaraj Chetty, Charles Cousins, Jamie Crawford, Andrew Feinstein, Diana Ferrus, Cheryl Gillwald, Lisa Jardine, Jackie Kay, Tessa Lewin, Hugh McLean, Anne McClintock, Don McNicol, Bill Mitchell, John O'Connell, Maggie Pearlstine,

Theresa Raizenberg, Janine Rawson, Jacqueline Rose, Todd Rubin, James Rycroft, Kamila Shamsie, Karen Simmons, Louise Ellison-Shaljean, Simone Sultana, Goniwe Stuurman, Chris Woods, and Brian Thomson.

On legal questions I have been advised by Justice Edwin Cameron and Sadakat Kadri, to whose intellectual insight, rigor, and generosity I owe a great many thanks.

With ever present memory to Thelma Lewis, Roy Porter, and Burhan Tufail, who gave valuable support and insight.

Enkosi, dankie, thank you to Saartjie's Sistawives: Lucilla Blankenberg, Deena Bosch, Nonkosi Khumalo, and Sipho Mthathi.

Many thanks to Mark Gevisser.

Much gratitude and many thanks to David Ebershoff and Caroline Michel.

Special thanks to Tanya Hudson, Rob Nixon, Jeanette Winterson, Jack Lewis, Zackie Achmat, and Sox.

Thanks to my parents, Helmut, Sarah, and my mother, Karin; and thank you to my very special sister Karen.

To my father, Don Holmes, who gave me my education. With appreciation, love, and esteem.

Finally and most importantly my deepest thanks to my partner, Jerry Brotton, for all things and for all we share—past, present, and the best of the future yet to come. It was Jerry who first encouraged me to tell Saartjie's story, who put up with me whilst she led the dance, who supports me in all things and shares the journey through thick and thin, who makes life fun, and whose brilliant books, mind, and unmatchable personality are a constant inspiration to me. I dedicate this book to Jerry: with infinite variety, admiration, and love always.

NOTES

2 *be but short* · Daniel Lysons, *Collectanea; or a Collection of Advertisements and Paragraphs from Newspapers, Relating to Various Subjects,* vol. Iii, unpublished scrapbook, British Library.

3 *inches in height* · George Cuvier, *Report on Observations Made on the Body of a Woman Known in Paris and in London as the Hottentot Venus* (Paris: Memoires du Musée National d'Histoire Naturelle, 1817).

5 *"was . . . 'nattral.' "* · This and all citations below from this episode between Saartjie, Mathews, Cesars, and Kemble are from Anne Mathews, *Memoirs of Charles Mathews, Comedian,* vol. 4 (London, 1839), pp. 133–37.

5 *"poor creature, no!"* · As well as an actor, Kemble was an innovative manager. In 1788, he introduced live animals to the London stage for the first time.

5 *" 'O ma Babba!' "* · Originating from Africa and the Indian subcontinent, *Baba* is now a common form of address across the world. In languages with Nguni roots, as spoken by Saartjie, *Baba* is the term of respect reserved for fathers, elders, and men of a certain age and status. Khoisan shares a common root with Xhosa and Zulu. In Xhosa, *utata* means father. It is notable that Kemble, an actor known for his deliberate enunciation, correctly interprets this term that Mathews finds "unintelligible." In Hindi, which also influenced sub-Saharan African languages, *Baba* is a term of endearment. It means father or grandfather, but in common usage may be applied to people of any age about whom one feels particular affection and respect.

6 *received an invitation* · Anna H. Smith, "Still More About the Hotten-

tot Venus," *Africana Notes and News* 26, no. 3 (September 1984), Africana Society, Africana Museum, City of Johannesburg.

7 *Admittance 2s each* · *The Morning Herald,* September 20, 1810, p. 1.

CHAPTER 2 · M TAI !NUERRE—"MY MOTHER'S COUNTRY"

8 *M Tai !Nuerre—"My Mother's Country"* · This /Xam phrase, meaning "home," is from a well-known San story called "The Moon and the Hare." See Janette Deacon and Thomas Dowson, eds., *Voices from the Past: /Xam Bushmen and the Bleek and Lloyd Collection* (Johannesburg: Witwatersrand University Press, 1996), p. 191.

8 *her first birthday* · Examination of the Hottentot Venus, November 27, 1810, Affidavit, KB1/36, part 4, King's Bench, Court Records, The National Archives, Kew, Surrey, England.

9 *since prehistoric times* · Despite strenuous arguments to the contrary by nineteenth-century ethnographers, anthropological evidence clearly shows that the Khoekhoen and the San emerged from one people, and were not separate races. The Khoekhoen became a distinct class in the late Stone Age, when their society shifted from hunting and gathering to animal husbandry and pastoralism. While the Khoekhoen became farmers, the San retained their seasonally shifting bush culture. Over time, the San, whose livelihood was more precarious, were employed as servants, hunters, and soldiers by the cattle-rich Khoekhoen. The collective term Khoisan (Khoi or Khoe, and San) is now used when speaking of the long shared history of South Africa's first peoples, to explicitly reject both antiquated colonial notions about "Bushmen" and "Hottentots," and the freight of racism inextricable from the etymology of these terms. See Shula Marks, "Khoisan Resistance to the Dutch in the Seventeenth and Eighteenth Centuries," *Journal of African History* 13, no. 1 (1972), pp. 55–80, reference p. 57.

9 *or "clicks"* · For a more detailed account of the Khoisan language, see Megan Biesele, "Stories and Storage: Transmission of Ju/'Hoan Knowledges and Skills," paper presented at the Ninth International Conference on Hunting and Gathering Societies, Edinburgh, Scotland, September 9–13, 2002.

10 *and fixed settlement* · In reality, the divisions were arbitrary; a

Khoekhoen without cattle who reverted to hunting and gathering became a Bushman, and a Bushman who worked for white settlers was seen as Khoekhoen.

10 *of Khoisan people* · See Marks, "Khoisan Resistance to the Dutch in the Seventeenth and Eighteenth Centuries," pp. 55–80, reference p. 55. These stereotypes have been extensively documented in academic work on this history of negative representation. See for example Londa Schiebinger, *Nature's Body: Gender in the Making of Modern Science* (Boston: Beacon Press, 1993), and Z. S. Strother, "Display of the Body Hottentot," in *Africans on Stage: Studies in Ethnological Show Business*, ed. Bernth Lindfors (Bloomington & Indianapolis: Indiana University Press, 1999), pp. 1–61.

10 *of ethnic origin* · "Hottentot" was the term by which Saartjie came to be defined, but she was also frequently described as a "Bushman," and sometimes, by European scholars perplexed by their own inventions, a "Bushman-Hottentot." These terms were in common usage in Saartjie's childhood, and were part of her own vocabulary. Conversing in Afrikaans, she used the Dutch-Afrikaans variant of "Bosmen" (also "Bosjesman") to describe the San people she knew from childhood. For example, see Examination of the Hottentot Venus, November 27, 1810.

10 *trekboers* · poor, wandering livestock farmers who migrated inland away from the Western Cape toward the frontiers of the colony. Descendants primarily of Dutch, French Huguenot, German, and Scots settlers frequently intermingled or intermarried with indigenous Khoisan, Malays, and slaves from the Cape.

10 *and farm lands* · In ancient times, the Xhosa spearheaded the expansion of the Nguni peoples into the African subcontinent, a migration that originated in the Cameroon. The Xhosa and the Zulu, also part of this movement, were the two key groups who settled in what is now known as South Africa. Archaeological research suggests that the earliest presence of Nguni Iron-Age pastoralists in southeastern Africa can be dated to around the seventh and eighth centuries. Xhosa polity and society were structured around vast cattle herds, strict codes of hospitality, a disposition to peace and negotiation rather than war, and fierce loyalty to their chiefs, who led democratic decision-making and judicial processes. The principal cultural characteristics of the Xhosa

suggest Semitic origins, and many believe they are derived from Mosaic law. Over centuries, the Xhosa-speaking nations diversified into many interrelated chiefdoms and peoples, structured around the key divisions into Pondo, Tembu, and Xhosa. The Xhosa settled in the area now known as the Eastern Cape, and emerged into a number of clans, the chief groups among them being the Gcaleka, Ngika, Ndlambe, Dushane, Qayi, Ntinde, and, of Khoisan origin, the Gqunkhwebe. Between 1670 and 1770 two major schisms occurred in Xhosa society. These splits, and the resulting authority crisis, were the cause of the westward migration towards the Fish River by breakaway chiefdoms. See Noël Mostert, *Frontiers: The Epic of South Africa's Creation and the Tragedy of the Xhosa People* (London: Jonathan Cape, 1992); Hermann Giliomee, "The Eastern Frontier, 1770–1812," in *The Shaping of South African Society, 1652–1820,* eds. Richard Elphick and Hermann Giliomee (London: Maskew, Miller, Longman, 1979), pp. 291–337; Ben Maclennan, *A Proper Degree of Terror: John Graham and the Cape's Eastern Frontier* (Johannesburg: Raven Press, 1986).

11 *farms surrounding them* · Named after the rivers running through them: the Gamtoos, the Kabeljouws, and the Loerie.

11 *to one another* · Giliomee, "The Eastern Frontier 1770–1812," in *The Shaping of South African Society, 1652–1820,* pp. 291–337, reference p. 297.

11 *read or write* · Khoisan was an oral language, and Saartjie was already twelve years old when the first Khoisan spelling book was printed by the London Missionary Society, but she would have had no knowledge of, or access to, it.

11 *tricky to master* · Travelers and, later, anthropologists, claimed that this instrument was played only by Khoisan men.

11 *for a fixed fee* · For this account of Khoekhoen employment on the eastern frontier, see Richard Elphick, "The Khoisan to c.1770," in *The Shaping of South African Society, 1652–1820,* pp. 3–33, reference p. 27.

12 *"from the interior to the Cape"* · Examination of the Hottentot Venus, November 27, 1810.

12 *and Khoi servants* · Marks, "Khoisan Resistance to the Dutch," p. 73.

12 *exacerbated the conflict* · Nigel Penn, "The Frontier in the Western Cape," in *Papers in the Prehistory of the Western Cape,* eds. John Parking-

ton and Martin Hall (Oxford: BAR International Series 332, 1987). See also Robert Shell, *Children of Bondage: A Social History of the Slave Society at the Cape of Good Hope, 1652–1838* (Johannesburg: Witwatersrand University Press, 1994), pp. 30–32.

12 *"them as bondsmen"* · Report from the Select Committee on Aborigines (British Settlements) with the Minutes of Evidence, Appendix and Index, London, House of Commons, June 26, 1837, p. 28, cited in Shell, *Children of Bondage*, p. 32.

12 *pair of shoes* · See Caitlin Davies, *The Return of El Negro: The Compelling Story of Africa's Unknown Soldier* (London: Penguin, 2003), p. 13.

13 *or eighteen* · See Examination of the Hottentot Venus, November 27, 1810; and Inventoris Van Opgaafrolle, Kaapstad en Kaapse Distrik, Opgaafrolle 1/5 (1807), Government Archives, Cape Town, J41, p. 70.

13 *"barbaric"* · Anon., "La Vénus Hottentote," *Journal des Dames et des Modes* (Paris), January 25, 1815, pp. 37–40.

13 *many warring factions* · The cattle runs divided between legal trade with the Dutch East India Company and illegal trade with trekboers and settler farmers.

13 *raiding operations* · Marks, "Khoisan Resistance to the Dutch," p. 67; Mostert, *Frontiers: The Epic of South Africa's Creation;* Giliomee, "The Eastern Frontier, 1770–1812," pp. 291–337; Maclennan, *A Proper Degree of Terror.*

14 *"greatly in demand"* · Anon., "La Vénus Hottentote," pp. 37–40.

14 *"entered most deeply"* · Ibid., p. 37.

14 *"their footsteps"* · Ibid., p. 39.

14 *reed flute* · The guitar, or *ramakib*, was made out of hollowed wood, with a calabash or touch board attached to one end, over which were drawn the strings; the *goura* was a stringed wind instrument common to the Southern Khoisan, and reed flutes are reed flutes everywhere. For an introduction to Khoisan musical instruments, see I. Schapera, *The Khoisan Peoples of South Africa: Bushmen and Hottentots* (London: Routledge & Kegan Paul, 1930), pp. 206–7; and Deirdre Hansen, "Bushman Music: Still an Unknown," in *Miscast: Negotiating the Presence of the Bushmen,* ed. Pippa Skotnes (Cape Town: University of Cape Town Press, 1996), pp. 297–305.

14 *"sea and the clouds"* · Anon., "La Vénus Hottentote," p. 40.

14 *of her life* · It can be seen in most of the images produced of her during her lifetime.

15 *"eyes to heaven"* · Anon., "La Vénus Hottentote," p. 38.

15 *adopted niece* · Asked how old she was when she was taken to Cape Town, Saartjie contradicted herself. First, she said that she was so very young that she could not remember, but then categorically stated that she lived in Cape Town for three years, until she left aged twenty-one. These factual fault lines reveal something of the distress of Saartjie's inner life. Trauma may have made her memory evasive and protective, and she later had reason to be cautious and opaque about these events. She also may not have been exactly sure when she was born.

15 *Saartjie's youth* · See Examination of the Hottentot Venus, November 27, 1810.

CHAPTER 3 · **CITY OF LOST CHILDREN**

17 *the Cape Peninsula* · Examination of the Hottentot Venus, November 27, 1810, Affidavit, KB1/36, part 4, The National Archives (TNA, formerly Public Record Office), London. Saartjie never specified their mode of travel. The available options were to travel overland, or take a ship's passage from Algoa Bay to Cape Town. As an itinerant trader, Pieter Cesars was most likely to travel overland.

17 *monkey ropes* · lianas.

17 *"comers and goers"* · Philip Edwards, ed., *The Journals of Captain Cook 1768–1779* (London: Penguin Books, 1999), p. 205.

18 *in 1815* · The Reverend John Campbell, London Missionary Society, unpublished sketchbook, Africana Museum, Johannesburg. See Percival Kirby, "The 'Hottentot Venus' of the Musée de L'Homme, Paris," *Suid-Afrikaanse Joernaal van Wetenskap* (July 1954), p. 321.

18 pondoks · This Malayan word for house found its way into kitchen-Dutch, then later Afrikaans, from the earliest settlement of the Cape. *Pondokkie* is still used in Afrikaans to signify a small, informal, temporary structure.

18 lyf-eigen-slaven · See the 1807 census, Inventoris Van Opgaafrolle, Kaapstad en Kaapse Distrik, Opgaafrolle 1/5 (1807), Government Archives, Cape Town, J41, p. 70.

18 *"nursery maid"* · Examination of the Hottentot Venus, November 27, 1810.

18 *and shelter only* · Legislative changes introduced in 1809 made it compulsory to pay Hottentot servants a proper wage.

18 *"born in this remote corner"* · Will of Hendrik Cesars and Anna Catharina Staal, August 13, 1805, MOOC 7/1/61, no. 57 (1811), Government Archives, Cape Town. All citations are from an original translation by Robert Symonds and Rachel Holmes.

18 *married in 1805* · Ibid. Anna Catharina's parents are recorded as Elisabeth Jacobse and Hendrik Staal, but there is no record of Hendrik and Pieter's parents.

18 *expected to raise children* · Ibid.

18 *the Orphan Chamber* · Recorded as "one daughter under the age of 25" in the Inventoris Van Opgaafrolle, p. 70.

18 *adopt a free child* · The Register of Wards of the Orphan Chamber starts in 1825. There are no known lists of orphans adopted from the Orphan Chamber during the period 1805 to 1808. As Shell points out, the Cape Town Orphan Chamber was created in the seventeenth century to protect the needs and interests of free orphans. (There was no provision for slave orphans until 1815.) From 1652 to 1819, the descent systems for both slavery and freedom at the Cape were matrilineal. This applied to everyone: slaves, free blacks, and free citizens. See Robert Shell, *Children of Bondage: A Social History of the Slave Society at the Cape of Good Hope, 1652–1838* (Johannesburg: Witwatersrand University Press, 1994), p. 128 and p. 217.

19 *a city of lost children* · See Shell, *Children of Bondage*, pp. 81–3; pp. 128–130.

19 *of 1807* · See Inventoris Van Opgaafrolle. On August 10, 1807, the government issued a proclamation ordering a census, to take place until December 1, covering Cape Town and surrounding districts. The census shows the exact composition of the Cesarses' household at the time that Saartjie was working as their nursemaid. The age of the three male "Hottentot" servants and the two male "life slaves" is given as over sixteen. Only the names of the heads of the household were listed. Children, Hottentot servants, and slaves were simply listed by numbers.

19 *no female slaves* · One of the male slaves was named January of Mozambique. See 1811 codicil to 1805 will: "our slave boy, January of

Mozambique, after we have both died, must be released from the estate—and moreover, a sum of fifty rijks daalders (=125 guilders) shall be paid to him from the estate." Will of Hendrik Cesars and Anna Catharina Staal, August 13, 1805.

19 *other, richer groups* · Shell, *Children of Bondage*, pp. xxxii–xxxiii.

19 *an illiterate manservant* · Hendrik testified that he could not write in his and Anna Catharina's will. Will of Hendrik Cesars and Anna Catharina Staal, August 13, 1805. In the 1810 codicil to the will, the registering clerk recorded: "This is the mark of the first appearer [Hendrik Cesars] who testified that he could not write."

19 *settler families* · See C. J. de Villiers, adapted by C. Pama, *Genealogies of Old South African Families*, vols. 1–3 (Cape Town: AA Balkema, 1966); D. F. Du Toit Malherbe, Family Register of the South African Nation (Stellenbosch: 1966); R. T. J. Lombard, *Handbook for Genealogical Research in South Africa* (Pretoria: 1990); Peter Philip, *British Residents at the Cape: Biographical Records of 4800 Pioneers* (Cape Town: David Philip, 1981).

19 *from the 1700s* · For examples, see "Caesars van Mosambique," Lyst der Transporten van Plaatzen, Slaaven, & mitsgaders Actens van Cesfie gepasfeerd in den jaare 1800, no. 587, tot 748, NCD 1/41, no. 601, February 1, 1800; and "Caesar from Batavia," Court of Justice Records, CJ796, no. 42, 1794.

19 *in the eighteenth century* · See C. Pama, *Die Groot Afrikaanse Familie-Naamboek* (Johannesburg and Cape Town: Human & Rousseau, 1983); and *Genealogies of Old South African Families*, vol. 3.

20 *transported to the Cape* · See Shell, *Children of Bondage*, p. 432.

20 *not exist* · For the most comprehensive analysis of the history of slave orphans, and orphan estimates for the child slave population at the Cape in the early nineteenth century, see Shell, *Children of Bondage*, pp. 85–134.

20 *their own fertility* · Ibid., pp. 304–5.

21 *renegade miscreant* · See the colonial office correspondence concerning Dunlop, CO22, 1810, Government Archives, Cape Town.

21 *Cape Town garrison* · Examination of the Hottentot Venus, November 27, 1810.

21 *and battle uniforms* · Typically, white trousers and a scarlet tunic topped by a gaily bedecked turban.

21 *their military duties* · Drummers were the beat keepers of the march, and almost all battle signals were performed on the drum. In garrison, drummers were the company's, regiment's, brigade's, or army's clock: commands on the drum included the call to camp duty, church call, and the call to the parade ground.

22 *Hendrik and Anna* · Examination of the Hottentot Venus, November 27, 1810.

22 *monthly wage* · Two pounds, nineteen shillings, and fivepence; see Army Paylists, WO12/9399 and WO12/9400, National Archives, London.

22 *was Irish* · *Morning Herald,* November 29, 1810, p. 3.

22 *"married to a Negro"* · Georges Cuvier, *Report on Observations Made on the Body of a Woman Known in Paris and London as the Hottentot Venus* (Paris: Memoires du Musée National d'Histoire Naturelle, 1817).

22 *an Nguni volunteer* · See Major G. Tylden, *The Armed Forces of South Africa,* City of Johannesburg Africana Museum, Frank Connock Publication no. 2 (Johannesburg: Trophy Press, 1982).

23 *are in perfection* · Letter from William Jones to Rev. B. E. Sparke, Cape Town, September 30, 1796, Bowyer Sparke Papers, Norfolk Record Office, UPC, 316/1.

23 *"The child is since dead."* · Examination of the Hottentot Venus, November 27, 1810.

CHAPTER 4 · STOWAWAY

25 *legally indentured* · See Sampie Terreblanche, *A History of Inequality in South Africa 1652–2002* (Scottsville: University of Natal Press, 2002), pp. 181–85.

25 *their judicial status* · Ibid., pp. 183–84.

26 *"general imbecile state"* · Sir Edward Hyde East, "The Case of the Hottentot Venus," *Reports of Cases argued and determined in the Court of King's Bench,* vol. 13 (London: A. Strahan, 1811), p. 195.

26 *28 Wale Street* · African Court Calendar (Cape Town: Government Printing Office, 1810), Z/1 1/12, Government Archives, Cape Town.

26 *in August 1803* · Colonel William Johnston, ed., *Roll of Commissioned Officers in the Medical Service of the British Army who served on full pay within the period between the accession of George II and the formation of the*

Royal Army Medical Corps, 20 June 1727 to 23 June 1898 (Scotland: Aberdeen University Press, 1917), p. 97.

26 *surgeon of the Slave Lodge* · The African Court Calendar, 1808, 1809, 1810 (Cape Town: Government Printing Office, 1808, 1809, 1810), ZI/1/12, Government Archives, Cape Town; George McCall Theal, *Records of the Cape Colony,* vol. 8 (Cape Town: Government of the Cape Colony, 1901), p. 140; and Percy Laidler and Michael Gelfland, *South Africa: Its Medical History, 1652–1898* (Cape Town: Struik, 1971), p. 237.

26 *short of resources* · Letter from C. G. Hohne to His Excellency, Dupré, Earl Caledon, Governor of the Cape, June 24, 1810, CO2450, section 8, no. 16, Government Archives, Cape Town.

27 *"Hottentot Women"* · Letters from Dr. Hussey to HM Fiscal J. Van Ryneveld, March 1 and March 8, 1808, CO22, no. 13, Government Archives, Cape Town.

27 *from the troops* · Letter from Dr. Hussey to HM Fiscal J. Van Ryneveld, December 2, 1808, CO22, no. 13, Government Archives, Cape Town.

27 *"of those people"* · Memorial of A. Dunlop to His Excellency, Dupré, Earl of Caledon, Governor and Commander in Chief of the Cape of Good Hope, and its Dependencies, CO3875, vol. 1, 1810, no. 79, Government Archives, Cape Town.

27 *sum of money* · In 1806 the value of one *rix-dollar* was four English shillings. Over the next nineteen years the value declined to one shilling and sixpence in 1825. Economic historians concur that there is no agreed historical exchange value between *rix-dollars* and contemporary currency; put simply, it was a large amount.

27 *"altogether inadmissible"* · Letter to Captain Forster from William Hussey MD, January 25, 1810, CO22, no. 13, Government Archives, Cape Town.

27 *"to his situation"* · Both quotes are from Letter from General Grey to Lord Caledon, January 26, 1810, CO22, no. 13, Government Archives, Cape Town.

28 *its exotica* · For a fuller account of this history, see Patricia Fara, *Sex, Botany & Empire* (Cambridge: Icon Books, 2003).

29 *"Boy hereafter"* · Henry Alexander to Alexander Dunlop, February 5, 1810, Lord Caledon Letter Book, July 19, 1809, to January 25, 1810, CO4827, Government Archives, Cape Town, p. 410.

29 *"he returns"* · Alexander Dunlop to Lord Caledon, March 16, 1810, with enclosure from Thomas Ord, Custom House, CO22, no. 29, Government Archives, Cape Town.

29 *by sickness* · Alexander Dunlop to Henry Alexander, March 7, 1810, CO22, no. 25, Government Archives, Cape Town.

29 *Daniel Tack* · *The Cape Town Gazette, & African Advertiser,* vol. 5, Saturday, March 10, 1810, no. 217; and Records of Arrivals in Table Bay, PC3/1, Government Archives, Cape Town.

30 *"bound to England"* · Henry Alexander to Alexander Dunlop, Lord Caledon Letter Book, February 24, 1810, to December 31, 1810, CO4828, Government Archives, Cape Town, p. 48.

30 *their universal heir* · This clause also stipulated the release of January of Mozambique from the estate on their death, and bequeathed him a sum of 50 *rix-dollars* (125 guilders), Will of Hendrik Cesars and Anna Catharina Staal, August 13, 1805, MOOC 7/1/61, no. 57 (1811), Government Archives, Cape Town.

30 *April 1, 1810* · *The Cape Town Gazette, & African Advertiser,* April 7, 1810, vol. 5, no. 221, p. 1.

30 *troop ship* · Royal Navy Ship Records, Navy Lists. *Diadem*'s remaining musters for the period are at The National Archives, Kew, Admiralty Records, ADM37/4993 and ADM37/2754. *Diadem* had spent 1809 plying between Simon's Bay and Table Bay provisioning the garrison and moving personnel. In service, *Diadem* could hold a complement of up to five hundred men.

30 *"the spotted camelopard"* · Percy Bysshe Shelley, "The Witch of Atlas" (1820).

30 *to be newsworthy* · See "The Camelopardalis," *The Sporting Magazine,* 37, no. 218 (November 1810), pp. 81–82.

31 *Admiralty records* · The musters begin again on June 20, 1810, when *Diadem* began wages and sea-victualling at Chatham; see ADM37/2754.

31 *"her back rich"* · *The Examiner,* November 28, 1810, no. 152, p. 768.

31 *"belonging to her"* · Examination of the Hottentot Venus, November 27, 1810, Affidavit, KB1/36, part 4, King's Bench, Court Records, The National Archives, Kew.

31 *their expense* · Examination of the Hottentot Venus, November 27, 1810.

32 *Table Mountain* · 3,563 feet above sea level.

CHAPTER 5 · **VENUS RISING**

33 *in May 1810* · Royal Navy Ship Records, Navy Lists, The National Archives, Kew, ADM37/2754.

34 *"brilliant light"* · Arthur Irwin Dasent, *The History of St. James's Square and the Foundation of the West End of London* (London: Macmillan, 1895).

35 *popularly regarded* · See Nicholas Thomas, *Discoveries: The Voyages of Captain Cook* (London: Penguin, 2003), and Patricia Fara, *Sex, Botany & Empire* (Cambridge: Icon Books, 2003).

35 *"amusement in London"* · Richard Altick, *The Shows of London* (Cambridge, Mass.: The Belknap Press of Harvard University Press, 1978), p. 235.

35 *"considerable value"* · Deposition to the Court of the King's Bench by William Bullock, November 21, 1810, The National Archives, Kew, KB 1/36, part 4.

35 *"a Hottentot Woman"* · Ibid.

35 *"Cape of Good Hope"* · Ibid.

35 *"of the woman"* · Ibid.

35 *"of great curiosity"* · Ibid.

35 *"to the public"* · Ibid.

35 *was six years* · See Examination of the Hottentot Venus, November 27, 1810, Affidavit, KB1/36, part 4, King's Bench, Court Records, The National Archives, Kew.

36 *James Cook* · Altick, *The Shows of London*, p. 235.

36 *"fine arts"* · *A Companion to Mr Bullock's Museum, containing a brief description of upwards of 7000 Natural and Foreign Curiosities* (London: Printed for the Proprietor by Henry Reynell, 1810), British Library, London, Mic.A.12582(3).

36 *appropriate environment* · Altick, *The Shows of London*, p. 237. Altick's account of Bullock corrects the many factual errors regarding Bullock and his museums contained in the first *Dictionary of National Biography*.

36 *of his museum* · *A Companion to Mr Bullock's Museum*, Mic.A.12582(3).

36 *"of the public"* · Deposition to the Court of the King's Bench by William Bullock, November 21, 1810.

36 *"body into disrepute"* · Andrew Gage and William Stearn, *A Bicentenary History of The Linnean Society of London* (London: Academic Press, 1988), p. 196.

37 *freak-show impresarios* · See Leslie Fiedler, *Freaks: Myths and Images of the Secret Self* (Harmondsworth, Middlesex: Penguin, 1981), and Altick, *The Shows of London*.

37 *a bowed lute* · This instrument was known to the Khoisan as a *mamokho-rang;* Europeans described it as a Jew's harp.

37 *"of her country"* · Georges Cuvier, *Report on Observations Made on the Body of a Woman Known in Paris and in London as the Hottentot Venus* (Paris: Memoires du Musée National d'Histoire Naturelle, 1817).

38 ONE SHILLING · *Punch*, September 4, 1847, cited in Richard Altick, *The Shows of London*.

38 *genuinely mottled* · Daniel Lysons, *Collectanea; or a Collection of Advertisements and Paragraphs from the Newspapers, Relating to Various Subjects,* vol. Ii, unpublished scrapbook, British Library.

38 *"Sicilian Fairy"* · See Altick, *The Shows of London*, and Anne Mathews, *Memoirs of Charles Mathews, Comedian*, vol. 4, (London: 1839), pp. 133–37.

38 *flying dragons* · John Thomas Smith, *An Antiquarian Ramble in the Streets of London*, vol. 1, ed. Charles Mackay (London: Richard Bentley, 1846), p. 28.

39 *a lot of scenery* · The fabulously successful Giant O'Brien, for example, had only a stool for his stage set. See Hilary Mantel, *The Giant O'Brien* (London: 4th Estate, 1998), and Altick, *The Shows of London*.

39 *"of South Africa"* · Kirby, "The Hottentot Venus," p. 57.

40 *"around her waist"* · This and the previous citation are from Examination of the Hottentot Venus, November 27, 1810.

40 *"greedy for generation"* · Aristotle's description of the pudenda of women. See Fiedler, *Freaks*, p. 138.

41 *summons of Cesars* · A Constant Reader, "The Female Hottentot," *The Examiner,* October 21, 1810, p. 653.

41 *"a fairly good ear"* · Cuvier, *Report on Observations Made on the Body of a Woman Known in Paris and in London as the Hottentot Venus*.

41 *and sashayed and sang* · Candace Allen, *Valaida: A Novel* (London: Virago, 2004), p. 159. This phrase is borrowed directly from Allen's exceptional novel, a work inspired by the historical legacy of black female performers. I am citing a novel because the performance arts of these singers and musicians are rarely described accurately or meaningfully in conventional history.

42 *a remarkable curiosity* · See Peter Fryer, *Staying Power: The History of Black People in Britain* (London: Pluto Press, 1984).

42 *about twenty thousand* · In 1772 the Lord Chief Justice's court accepted a figure of fifteen thousand black people in Britain. Granville Sharp thought the number was nearer twenty thousand. See Paul Edwards and James Walvin, *Black Personalities in the Era of the Slave Trade* (London: Macmillan, 1983). Peter Fryer suggests a more conservative figure of ten thousand; see *Staying Power*, p. 235.

43 *her equal* behind · *Morning Herald,* December 12, 1810, p. 3.

43 *who showed her legs* · Academic Yvette Abrahams has cogently argued the significance of this. In so doing she effectively challenges recent academic work that seeks to prove, erroneously, that Saartjie was never seen as an erotic object by white culture, but only as gross and abject. This misreading of the erotic is a result of scholarship that focuses only on sources from elite travel accounts, ethnography, and anthropology, and entirely ignores contemporary press and popular cultural sources. See Abrahams, "Images of Sara Bartman: Sexuality, Race, and Gender in Early-Nineteenth-Century Britain," in *Nation, Empire, Colony: Historicizing Gender and Race*, eds. Ruth Roach Pierson and Nupur Chaudhuri (Bloomington & Indianapolis: Indiana University Press, 1998), pp. 225–36.

44 *living specimens* · See Altick, *The Shows of London*, pp. 268–87.

45 *of natural productions* · *Morning Herald,* November 23, 1810, p. 3.

45 *"of savoury soup"* · This and the previous citation: *The Satirist, or, Monthly Meteor* 7, no. 3, (November 1, 1810) pp. 424–27.

46 *to the parlour* · Ibid.

46 *"the Hottentot protuberances"* · Ibid.

46 *"his grace's kind attentions"* · Ibid.

46 *"tink of dis country"* · *Morning Post,* November 9, 1810, p. 3.

47 *she sad one* · Ibid.

47 *around central London* · Examination of the Hottentot Venus, November 27, 1810.

CHAPTER 6 · **FREEWOMAN, OR SLAVE?**

48 *"when company was there"* · *The Examiner,* October 14, 1810, p. 9.

48 *"force her compliance"* · Ibid.

48 *"delayed no longer"* · *The Examiner,* October 9, 1810, p. 653.

48 *"chanced to laugh"* · *The Examiner,* October 14, 1810, p. 9.

48 *"sickness, servitude"* · Ibid.

48 *"musical instrument"* · Ibid.

48 *"wild as a beast"* · Ibid.

48 *willing to agree* · For audience complicity with Cesars's strategy for dealing with this episode, see *The Examiner,* October 14, 1810, p. 9.

49 *and mortifying sight* · Letter to the editor from Humanitas, "The Female Hottentot," *The Examiner,* October 21, 1810, p. 669.

49 *"commands of her keeper"* · "The Hottentot Venus," *The Sporting Magazine* 37, no. 218 (November 1810), pp. 81–82.

49 *"like a chained beast"* · Ibid.

50 *"ringleaders in the crime"* · Cited in Hugh Thomas, *The Slave Trade: The History of the Atlantic Slave Trade, 1440–1870* (London: Macmillan, 1997), p. 556.

50 *"improvement of Africa"* · African Institution Charter, Report of the Committee of the African Institution, General Meeting, July 15, 1807, rules and regulations, then adopted as constitution for the society; London, 1807, Freemason's Hall, Queen Street, Lincoln's Inn Fields, British Library, T87.

50 *"of the Slave Trade"* · Ibid.

50 *Samuel Whitbread* · Other founder members included the Reverend Thomas Gisborne; the bishops of London, Durham, Bath, and Wells; bankers Thomas Baring and R. Barclay; Henry Brougham; Lord Headley; Nicholas Vansittard; Sir Philip Francis; Sir Samuel Romilly; the viscounts Howick and Valenta; and the Duke of Montague.

50 *"eager and adventurous traffic"* · George Harrison, Some Remarks on a Communication from William Roscoe to the Duke of Gloucester, March 20, 1809, as stated in the appendix of the third report of the African Institution (London, 1810), British Library 899 c22, p. 7.

50 *"upon the African race"* · Ibid., p. 5.

50 *that it supplied* · Thomas, *The Slave Trade,* p. 562.

50 *abuses against abolition* · Such as, in 1814, rescuing a West Indian apprentice who had been found chained to his master's table and treated appallingly. See Peter Fryer, *Staying Power: The History of Black People in Britain* (London: Pluto Press, 1984), p. 228.

50 *"abominable traffic"* · See Thomas, *The Slave Trade,* p. 535.

51 *Middle Passage* · Ibid., p. 412.

51 *"the Hottentot Venus"* · *Morning Chronicle*, October 12, 1810, p. 3.

51 *"her own country"* · Sworn affidavit of Zachary Macaulay, Thomas Gisborne Babington, and Peter Van Wageninge, Serjeant's Inn, Chancery Lane, London, October 17, 1810, KB/36, The National Archives, Kew.

51 *"no further satisfaction"* · All citations from this passage, ibid.

52 *"all situations, Slavery"* · *Morning Chronicle*, October 12, 1810, p. 3.

52 *"any other man living"* · In 1833, on the passing of the Emancipation Bill, Charles Buxton wrote to Macaulay, "My sober and deliberate opinion is, that you have done more towards this consummation than any other man." This and previous citations in the paragraph are found in Ernest Marshall Howse, *Saints in Politics: The "Clapham Sect" and the Growth of Freedom* (London: George Allen and Unwin, 1952), p. 22.

53 *"£500 per annum"* · Maurice Quinlan, *Victorian Prelude: A History of English Manners, 1700–1830* (London: Frank Cass, 1965), pp. 203–204.

53 *"books and prints"* · Ibid., pp. 205–6.

53 *of women's rights* · See Catherine Hall, *White, Male and Middle Class: Explorations in Feminism and History* (Cambridge & Oxford: Polity Press, 1998).

53 *"idiosyncrasies and abnormalities"* · Bernth Lindfors, " 'The Hottentot Venus': and other African attractions in nineteenth-century England," *Australasian Drama Studies* 1, no. 2 (1982), p. 84.

54 *"deprived of her liberty"* · All citations from this passage: Macaulay, Babington, Van Wageninge, Affidavit, October 17, 1810.

54 *"compelled, as a stranger"* · *Morning Chronicle*, October 13, 1810, p. 3.

54 *"satisfaction of the public"* · Ibid.

54 *"greatest kindness and tenderness"* · Ibid.

54 *Saartjie's passport* · *Morning Chronicle*, October 17, 1810, p. 3.

54 *"their coming on board"* · Ibid.

55 *"should be punished"* · Ibid.

55 *"by force"* · *Morning Chronicle*, October 23, 1810, p. 4.

55 *"my conduct"* · Ibid.

55 *"make the angels weep"* · Letter to the editor from Humanitas, *The Examiner*, October 21, 1810, p. 669.

55 *"vice or misfortune"* · This and previous citation, ibid.

55 *"who now attends"* · *Morning Chronicle*, October 23, 1810, p. 4.

55 *"to do with her"* · Affidavit of William Bullock, Court of the King's Bench, Westminster, November 21, 1810, KB1/36, part 4, NAL.

56 *"or a Dwarf &c, &c?"* · *Morning Chronicle*, October 23, 1810, p. 4.

56 *"be made to appear"* · *Morning Chronicle*, October 24, 1810, p. 3.

56 *Sir Vikar* · *A Ballad: The storie of the Hottentot Ladie and her lawfull Knight, who essaied to release her out of captivitie, and what my lordes the judges did therein* (London: James Gillet, Printer, Hatton Garden, 1810), Daniel Lysons, *Collectanea*, vol. Iii.

57 *to serve the HOTTENTOT* · Ibid.

CHAPTER 7 · THE CASE OF THE HOTTENTOT VENUS

58 *Sir Simon Le Blanc* · Le Blanc, appointed Justice of the King's Bench in 1799, was a senior barrister.

58 *habeas corpus* · The writ of habeas corpus ("that you have the body") is a process for securing the liberty of the subject by affording an effective means of immediate release from unlawful or unjustifiable detention whether in prison or in private custody. It is a prerogative writ by which the Sovereign has a right to inquire into the causes for which any of her subjects are deprived of their liberty. By it the High Court and the judges of that court, at the instance of the subject aggrieved, command the production of that subject, and inquire into the cause of his imprisonment. If there is no legal justification for the detention, the party is ordered to be released. See Halsbury's *Laws of England*, 4th ed., 2001 reissue, Vol. 1, ed. Lord Mackay of Clashfern (London: Butterworths, 2001), pp. 366–402; Earl Jowitt, *Dictionary of English Law* (London: Sweet and Maxwell, 1959), pp. 886–87.

58 *"their embarkation"* · *Morning Chronicle*, October 24, 1810.

58 *"right of humanity"* · "The Female Hottentot," *The Examiner*, October 21, 1810, p. 669.

58 *"her Country and friends"* · Sworn affidavit of Zachary Macaulay, Thomas Gisborne Babington, and Peter Van Wageninge, Serjeant's Inn, Chancery Lane, London, October 17, 1810, KB/36, PRO, Kew, London.

58 *"her native land"* · A Constant Reader (anon.), "The Female Hottentot," *The Examiner*, October 14, 1810, p. 653. The attribution of this

letter is uncertain. It is not Macaulay (see his response in the following issue, October 21, p. 669), but the concluding remarks regarding the benefits of a missionary education and voluntary repatriation clearly indicate someone from, or closely allied to, the Clapham Sect. The most likely candidates are Haldane and Hannah More.

59 *would be exhibited* · This and previous citations from Macaulay, Babington, Van Wageninge, Affidavit, October 17, 1810.

59 *"no art is practised"* · Ibid.

59 *"as free as the English"* · *Morning Chronicle*, October 13, 1810, p. 3.

59 *"worse than Egyptian bondage"* · "The Female Hottentot," *The Examiner*, October 21, p. 669.

59 *"burst her fetters"* · Letter to *The Examiner*, Sunday, October 21, 1810, p. 669.

59 *King's Bench* · For the history of the King's Bench court and its role in the machinery of justice, see Stanley de Smith and Rodney Brazier, *Constitutional and Administrative Law* (London: Penguin, 1998), pp. 359–87; and A. W. Bradley and K. D. Ewing, *Constitutional and Administrative Law* (Harlow: Addison Wesley Longman, 1997), pp. 408–455.

59 *November 24, 1810* · The Court of the King's Bench, the supreme common law court of England, is an appellate court headed by the king/queen or his/her personal representative, in this case the attorney general, the only person who could initiate legal proceedings on behalf of the crown. For the origins and history of the Court of the King's Bench see Erskine May, *The Constitutional History of England*, vol. 1 (London, New York, and Bombay: Longmans, Green, and Co., 1896); M. M. Knappen, *Constitutional and Legal History of England* (New York: Harcourt Brace, 1942); and John Hamilton Baker, *An Introduction to English Legal History* (London: Butterworths, 1990).

60 *as judge* · See Report of the Committee of the African Institution, General Meeting, July 15, 1807, rules and regulations, then adopted as constitution for the society; London, 1807, Freemason's Hall, Queen Street, Lincoln's Inn Fields, British Library, T87. Notably, Lord Ellenborough had earlier in the year also presided over William Cobbett's famous seditious libel trial. See Ben Wilson, *The Laughter of Triumph: William Hone and the Fight for the Free Press* (London: Faber & Faber, 2005), p. 76. I am grateful to Sadakat Kadri for explaining the significance of this to me.

60 *"a civilized country"* · "Law Report," *The Times* (London), November 26, 1810, p. 3.

60 *"friends of all humanity"* · Unless otherwise noted, this account of the court case and all citations for the hearings of November 26 and 29 are drawn from the following sources: "The Case of the Hottentot Venus," *The English Reports*, King's Bench Division, vol. 104, no. 33 (Oxford: Professional Books Ltd., reprint 1980), pp. 344–45; Sir Edward Hyde East, "The Case of the Hottentot Venus, Saturday, November 24, 1810", *Reports of Cases argued and determined in the Court of King's Bench*, vol. 13 (London: A. Strahan, 1811), pp. 195–96; "Law Report: Court of King's Bench, Saturday, November 24: The Hottentot Venus," *The Times* (London), November 26, 1810, p. 3, and November 29, 1810, p. 3; "Law Intelligence: Court of King's Bench, Saturday, November 24: The Hottentot Venus," *Morning Chronicle*, November 26, 1810, p. 3, and November 29, 1810, p. 3; "Law Report: Court of King's Bench, November 24: The Hottentot Venus," *Morning Herald*, November 26, 1810, p. 3, and November 29, 1810, p. 3; "The Hottentot Venus," *The Examiner*, October 21, 1810, p. 669. Manuscript copies of the affidavits of Saartjie Baartman, William Bullock, Zachary Macaulay, Thomas Babington, Peter Van Wageninge, and Alexander Dunlop are in the archive of the King's Bench, The National Archives, Kew.

60 *"he becomes free"* · David Brion Davis, *The Problem of Slavery in the Age of Revolution: 1770–1823* (Ithaca & London: Cornell University Press, 1975), p. 472.

61 *"if restrained of his liberty"* · Ibid., p. 473.

61 *"to breathe in"* · Ibid., p. 473.

61 *the Somerset case* · See *Somerset* v. *Stewart*, May 14, 1772, *The English Reports*, vol. 98, King's Bench Division, 28 (Oxfordshire: Professional Books Limited, 1909), pp. 499–510; Edmund Heward, *Lord Mansfield* (Chichester and London: Barry Rose Publishers, 1979), p. 143.

62 *workers at the Cape* · See Rachel Holmes, "Rainbow Afrikaans," *Prospect*, issue 98 (May 2004), pp. 78–79.

64 *"with his servant"* · Henry Alexander to Alexander Dunlop, Lord Caledon Letter Book, February 24, 1810, to December 31, 1810, CO4828, Government Archives, Cape Town, p. 48.

64 *"demand of her"* · This and all proceeding references to the contract

are from Prof. Verneau's translation, "Le centième anniversaire de la mort de Saartjie Bartmann," *L'Anthropologie*, vol. 27 (1916), p. 178.

65 *"magnificently attired"* · John Lord Campbell, *The Lives of the Chief Justices of England*, vol. 3 (London: John Murray, 1857), p. 161.

65 *free will and consent* · "The Case of the Hottentot Venus," *The English Reports*, vol. 104, King's Bench Division, 33 (Oxford: Professional Books, Ltd., reprint 1980), pp. 344–45; and Campbell, *The Lives of the Chief Justices of England*, p. 1661.

66 *Bordell v. Pickwick* · Charles Dickens, *The Pickwick Papers* (Oxford: Oxford University Press, 1987), pp. 466–67.

67 *"the seller receives nothing"* · Davis, *The Problem of Slavery* (1975), p. 489.

67 *"ingredients of slavery"* · Ibid.

68 *to their own bondage* · Ibid.

68 *of "Hottentots"* · The paternalism and utilitarian racism of this legislation can be seen from its opening justification: ". . . for the benefit of this Colony at large, it is necessary, that not only the Individuals of the Hottentot Nation, in the same manner as the other Inhabitants, should be subject to proper regularity in regard to their places of above and occupation, but also, that they should find an encouragement, for preferring entering the service of the Inhabitants, to leading an indolent life, by which they are rendered useless both for themselves, and the community at large." November 1, 1809, Official Proclamations, Caledon Papers, ZI1/1, Government Archives, Cape Town.

69 *costly, and risky* · They would first have had to prod the Crown to prosecute, and on their refusal to have obtained a nolle prosequi ("we shall no longer prosecute"), an entry made on the record by the prosecution stating that they would no longer pursue the matter; essentially, an admission on the part of the prosecution that some aspect of its case against the defendants had fallen apart. They could then have instituted a private prosecution. However, the case on behalf of the African Institution lacked the surety of being able to establish the burden of proof beyond a reasonable doubt, and the jury might have been inclined to be sympathetic with the accused, and so acquit. Given these potential complexities, there was far more control and security in the African Institution's pursuing the habeas corpus procedure.

69 *care of herself* · Angela Carter, *Black Venus* (London: Chatto & Windus, 1985), p. 20. In Carter's tale of Jeanne Duval, Baudelaire's mistress, Duval contemplates her status as a prostitute in Paris: "Seller and commodity in one, a whore is her own investment in the world and so she must take care of herself."

CHAPTER 8 · CACHE-SEXE

71 *after her departure* · *Morning Post*, April 30, 1811, p. 1.

71 *toured the provinces* · Bernth Lindfors, "The Afterlife of the Hottentot Venus," *Neohelican: Acta Comparat Litteraraum Universarum*, vol. 16, no. 2, Sept. 1989, pp. 293–301, reference p. 298.

71 *her popularity* · Bernth Lindfors, "The Bottom Line: African Caricature in Georgian England," *World Literature Written in English*, vol. 24, no. 1 (1984), pp. 43–51, reference pp. 49–50.

72 *London, Brighton, and Bath* · In "The Humours of Bartlemy Fair," Saartjie is described as one of the key attractions: "Here, here, the only booth in the fair, for the greatest curiosity in all the known world—the Vonderful and surprising Hottentot Wenus is here, who measures three yards and three quarters round." See "The Humours of Bartlemy Fair," *The Universal Songster*, vol. 1 (London: undated), pp. 118–19. A Cruikshank cartoon shows Saartjie on the playbill of summer entertainments in Brighton at the pavilion for the royal court. See Anna H. Smith, "Still More About the Hottentot Venus," *Africana Notes and News* 26, no. 3 (September 1984), Africana Society, Africana Museum, City of Johannesburg, pp. 95–98, this reference p. 97. "The Address of Jack Higginbottom in behalf of himself and the Hottentot Venus, to the Ladies of Bath," which poked merciless fun at the Clapham Saints, places Saartjie in Bath during the same summer.

72 *managed by Dunlop* · The diary of Rev. Dr. Laurence Hayes Halloran is cited in George McCall Theal, *Records of the Cape Colony*, vol. 8 (London: Printed for the government of the Cape Colony, 1897–1905); see also Peter Philip, *British Residents at the Cape: Biographical Records of 4800 Pioneers* (Cape Town: David Phillip, 1981), p. 162.

72 *Jos. Brookes Chaplain* · Register of the Collegiate and Parish Church of Christ, Manchester, December 1, 1811.

73 *"extraordinary occasion"* · *Cowdroys Manchester Gazette, and Weekly Advertiser,* December 14, 1811, p. 4.

73 *"visited by very few"* · Maurice Lenihan, *Limerick: Its History and Antiquities, Ecclesiastical, Civil and Military* (Cork: Mercier Press, 1967; orig. pub. 1886), p. 416; Bill Rolston and Michael Shannon, *Encounters: How Racism Came to Ireland* (Belfast: Beyond the Pale Publications, 2002), p. 70.

73 *of unknown causes* · Colonel William Johnston, *Roll of Commissioned Officers in the Medical Service of the British Army who served on full pay within the period between the accession of George II and the formation of the RAMC: 20 June 1727–23 June 1898* (Aberdeen: Aberdeen University Press, 1917), p. 97. Dunlop's Return of Service record was destroyed in bomb damage to the Public Records Office during World War II.

74 *last day of March* · Agreed by the allies on March 1, 1814, the Treaty of Chaumont bound the anti-Napoleon alliance for twenty years, and stated the objectives of victory as "an enlarged and independent Holland, a confederated Germany, an independent Switzerland, a free Spain under a Bourbon dynasty, and the restitution of the Italian states." See Asa Briggs, *The Age of Improvement* (London: Longmans, Green & Co., 1959), p. 159.

74 *"event in European history"* · See Herve Le Guyader, *Geoffroy Saint-Hilaire: A Visionary Naturalist* (Chicago: University of Chicago Press, 2004).

74 *colonnades of the Palais Royal* · As described by Elizabeth Barrett Browning in book 6 of *Aurora Leigh.* Elizabeth Barrett Browning, *Aurora Leigh,* ed. Margaret Reynolds (London: W. W. Norton & Company, 1996), p. 184.

75 *a certain Henry Taylor* · As Cesars could neither write nor speak French, he paid a letter writer to draft the correspondence and translate the text of Saartjie's publicity advertisements, brought from England.

75 *"conformation singulière"* · Henry Taylor to André Thouin, September 10, 1814, Correspondence et comptes rendus des assemblées des professeurs, National Archives, Paris. For a full transcription of the letter see Gerard Badou, *L'énigme de la Vénus Hottentote* (Paris: J. C. Lattès, 2000), p. 110.

75 *for the menagerie* · Badou, *L'énigme,* p. 115

75 *noted its contents* · See Franck Bourdier, "Georges Cuvier," *Dictionary of Scientific Biography*, vol. 3, ed. Charles Coulston Gillispie (New York: Charles Scribner's Sons, 1972), p. 524.

75 *"grew enormously fat"* · Ibid.

76 *the Hauzanana* · Strother points out that François Le Vaillant was the only traveler to write on the people he labelled the Hauzanana (a San group) in exclusive relation to whom he commented on and illustrated steatopygia. See Z. S. Strother, "Display of the Body Hottentot," *Africans on Stage: Studies in Ethnological Show Business*, ed. Bernth Lindfors (Bloomington & Indianapolis: Indiana University Press, 1999), p. 33. This literate awareness of the body of travel writing about the Cape raises interesting questions about the sources contributing to the authorship of the advertisements for the Hottentot Venus exhibition.

76 *Entry 3 fr.* · Affiches, Annonces et Avis Divers ou Journal Général de France, September 18, 1814, p. 15, Bibliothèque Nationale. The souvenir poster on offer was probably the ubiquitous aquatint by Frederick Christian Lewis.

77 *Dutch and English* · *Journal Général de France*, September 22, 1814, p. 13.

77 *dinners, parties* · "La Vénus Hottentote," *Journal des Dames et des Modes* (Paris), January 25, 1815, pp. 37–40.

77 *"charming"* · Ibid.

78 *"behind the curtains"* · Ibid.

78 *"fit of melancholy"* · Ibid.

78 *touching her clothes* · Ibid.

78 *"and Hottentot girls"* · Percival Kirby, "More about the Hottentot Venus," *Africana Notes and News* 10, no. 4 (Johannesburg, September 1953), pp. 124–34.

78 *"in gorgeous Hottentot costume"* · Ibid.

79 *is restored* · See Z. S. Strother, "Display of the Body Hottentot," pp. 1–61. Strother offers a concise reading of the racist negation of Saartjie as an object of desire in this cruel and misogynistic comedy.

79 *"a savage Venus"* · *Journal Général de France*, November 21, 1814, pp. 3–4.

79 *is something else* · Andrea Stuart, *Showgirls* (London: Jonathan Cape, 1996), p. 85.

79 *to maximize profits* · See announcement in the *Gazette de France*, October 28, 1814.

80 *a frenzied crowd* · Frank McLynn, *Napoleon: A Biography* (London: Jonathan Cape, 1997), pp. 606–7.

80 *"two thousand ryks dollars pure"* · Last will and testament of Anna Catharina Staal, widow of the late Hendrick Cesars, resident of Papendorp, August 2, 1841, Government Archives, Cape Town.

80 *January 22, 1815* · Affiches, Annonces et Avis Divers ou Journal Général de France, January 22, 1815. See also January 24, 26, and 27.

80 *"has changed owner"* · *Journal Général de France,* January 23, 1815.

81 *"a householder of Paris"* · See Percival Kirby, "The 'Hottentot Venus' of the Musée de L'Homme, Paris," *Suid-Afrikaanse Joernaal van Wetenskap* (July 1954), pp. 319–22.

81 *twenty-four hours' advance notice* · Affiches, Annonces et Avis Divers ou Journal Général de France, January 22, 1815. See also January 24, 26, 27, 28, and February 1 to February 8 inclusive.

CHAPTER 9 · **PAINTED FROM THE NUDE**

82 *on the left bank* · restored to its monarchist name following the return of the Bourbons. The botanical gardens continued to alternate between their republican and monarchist names until 1848, when they finally became the Jardin des Plantes for good.

82 *a panel of scientists and artists* · Records of this event emerged through scientific journals in the early twentieth century on the centenary of Saartjie's death. It was first referred to in Verneau, "Le centième anniversaire de la mort de Saartjie Bartmann," *L'Anthropologie,* vol. 27 (1916), and Jean Avalon, "Saartjie, La 'Vénus Hottentote,' " *Aesculape: Revue Mensuelle Illustrée—Organe Officiel de la Société Internationale d'Histoire de la Medicine,* vol. 16 (Paris: Société Internationale d'Histoire de la Medicine, 1926).

82 *after the show* · Georges Cuvier, *Report on Observations Made on the Body of a Woman Known in Paris and in London as the Hottentot Venus* (Paris: Memoires du Musée National d'Histoire Naturelle, 1817).

82 *in his diary* · These diary entries were discovered by Heather Ewing in the course of her research for her book on Smithson, founder of the Smithsonian Museum. I am grateful for her generosity in giving me these original references.

82 *"bounds of decency"* · The Diary of Sir Charles Blagden, October 9, 1814, Royal Society Archives.

82 *"have the apron"* · These citations all from the Diary of Sir Charles Blagden, January 10, 1815, Royal Society Archives.

83 *preserve the public order* · Letter from Étienne Geoffroy Saint-Hilaire to M. Boucheseiche, February 16, 1815, Archives de la préfecture de police de Paris. For a full transcript of the letter, see Gérard Badou, *L'énigme de la Vénus Hottentote* (Paris: J. C. Lattès, 2000), p. 133.

83 *governors of the Cape* · See Joseph-Philippe-François Deleuze, *Histoire et description du Muséum Royal d'Histoire Naturelle* (Paris: M. A. Royer, 1823), p. 106.

84 *in animals and plants* · For "freaks" and the science of teratology, see Leslie Fiedler, *Freaks: Myths and Images of the Secret Self* (Harmondsworth, Middlesex: Penguin, 1981); for Saint-Hilaire and the development of teratology, see Franck Bourdier, "Étienne Geoffroy Saint-Hilaire," in *Dictionary of Scientific Biography*, vol. 5, eds. Emil Fischer & Gottlieb Haberlandt (New York: Charles Scribner's Sons, 1972), pp. 355–58, and Michael Allin, *Zarafa* (London: Headline, 1998), pp. 134–35.

84 *"where no likeness exists"* · Deleuze, *Histoire et description du Muséum Royal d'Histoire Naturelle*, p. 174.

85 *of little interest to naturalists* · Henri de Blainville, "Sur une femme de la race hottentote," *Bulletin des Sciences par la Société Philomathique de Paris* (Paris: 1816), pp. 183–90.

86 *worn by even the most deformed* · See John Lempriere, *Lempriere's Classical Dictionary of Proper Names Mentioned in Ancient Authors Writ Large, With Chronological Table* (London: Routledge, 1986).

86 *"called the* Sinus pudoris*"* · Captain James Cook, *The Journals of Captain Cook 1768–1779*, ed. Philip Edwards (London: Penguin Books, 1999), p. 327. For a discussion of the apron in general and Saartjie Baartman in particular, see Carmel Schrire, "Native Views of Western Eyes," in *Miscast: Negotiating the Presence of the Bushmen*, ed. Pippa Skotnes (Cape Town: University of Cape Town Press, 1996), pp. 343–53, and Schrire, *Digging Through Darkness: Chronicles of an Archaeologist* (Charlottesville and London: University Press of Virginia, 1995), pp. 176–78.

87 *"cut from the body"* · R. Raven-Hart, *Before Van Riebeeck: Callers at South Africa from 1488 to 1652* (Cape Town: Struik, 1967), p. 152.

87 *the "famous apron"* · Cited in Z. S. Strother, "Display of the Body Hot-
tentot," in *Africans on Stage: Studies in Ethnological Show Business*, ed.
Bernth Lindfors (Bloomington & Indianapolis: Indiana University
Press, 1999), p. 21.

87 *women's genitals and neutralize desire* · Ibid., pp. 21–22.

87 *established in 1799* · Others among the founding group included the
biologists Lamarck, Jussieu, and Saint-Hilaire; the explorers Bou-
gainville and Le Vaillant; and the linguists Destutt de Tracy and
Sicard. See George Stocking, "French Anthropology in 1800," *Isis*
55:2, no. 180 (July 1964), pp. 134–50.

87 *examination of them* · Henri de Blainville, "Sur une femme de la race
hottentote," *Bulletin des Sciences par la Société Philomathique de Paris*
(Paris: 1816), pp. 183–90.

88 *"hatred for M. de Blainville"* · Ibid.

88 *however say with certainty* · Ibid.

88 *more particularly with pregnancy* · Ibid.

89 *"painted from the nude"* · Georges Cuvier, *Report on Observations.*

89 *one celestial, the other vulgar* · See Kenneth Clark, *The Nude* (Harmondsworth, Middlesex: Penguin, 1956), p. 64.

89 *an expression of deep sadness* · See Hugh Honour, *The Image of the Black
in Western Art*, vol. 4 (Cambridge, Mass.: Harvard University Press,
1989), pp. 54–55.

90 *a scientific journal in 1816* · *Bulletin des Sciences par la Société Philomathique de Paris.*

90 *burst into laughter* · Henri de Blainville, "Sur une femme de la race
hottentote," pp. 183–90, and Cuvier, *Report on Observations.*

91 *enacted his rage* · "And you should fear the vengeance of gods/Venus
who hates a stony heart, the wrath/The unforgetting wrath of Nemesis." Ovid, *Metamorphoses* (Oxford: Oxford University Press, 1986),
p. 346.

CHAPTER 10 · **THE DEATH OF VENUS**

92 *and animal tissue* · See Roy Porter, *The Greatest Benefit to Mankind: A
Medical History of Humanity from Antiquity to the Present* (London:
Harper Collins, 1997), p. 321.

92 *the second time* · Georges Cuvier, *Report on Observations Made on the Body*

of a Woman known in Paris and in London as the Hottentot Venus (Paris: Memoires du Musée National d'Histoire Naturelle, 1817).

93 *surgeons, and anatomists* · The most famous of course being Joseph Merrick, the Elephant Man. Frequently, the future donors were directly involved in the agreement, indemnified with the benefits of some much-needed cash for the remainder of their lifetime in exchange for their consent to give their dead bodies to science.

94 *"human knowledge"* · See Gérard Badou, *L'énigme de la Vénus Hottentote* (Paris: J. C. Lattès, 2000), pp. 152, 154.

94 *"the interest of public order"* · Letter from Geoffroy Saint-Hilaire to Prefect of Police, December 30, 1815, Collections officielles des ordonnances de Police: 1800–1848, Paris Police Archives. See Badou, *L'énigme*, pp. 152, 154.

94 *no legal right to dissect Saartjie* · See Badou, *L'énigme*, pp. 152, 154.

94 *the handover of the body* · Collections officielles des ordonnances de Police: 1800–1848, Paris Police Archives.

96 *this specimen* · Pierre Gratiolet, "Mémoire sur les plis cérébraux de l'homme et des primates," in Huxley's 1864 lecture series on "The Structure and Classification of the Mammalis," *Medical Times and Gazette* (October 1864).

96 *from slavery in America* · Huxley, "The Structure and Classification of the Mammalis."

96 *his Venus's genitalia* · For Cuvier's use of the possessive when referring to Saartjie, see Report on Observations.

96 *"entire skeleton"* · Cited in George Stocking, "French Anthropology in 1800," *Isis* 55: 2, no. 180 (July 1964), pp. 134–50.

96 *"infinitely precious"* · Ibid.

96 *"battles with savages"* · Ibid.

96 *"in any manner whatever"* · Ibid.

96 *"governed only by reason* · Ibid.

97 *"after a short illness of three days"* · "Paris News: 30th December," *Journal Général de France*, December 31, 1815, and Obituary, *Journal Général de France*, December 31, 1815.

97 *announced another* · "Nouvelles de Paris: La Vénus hottentote est morte," Obituary, *La Quotidienne*, January 1, 1816, p. 4.

97 *no other Olympus than a glass jar* · *Annales Politiques, Morales et Litteraires*, January 1, 1816.

97 *they needed no specification* · See Saul Dubow, *Scientific Racism in Modern South Africa* (Cambridge, England: Cambridge University Press, 1995), pp. 20–33, and Carmel Schrire, "Native Views of Western Eyes," in *Miscast: Negotiating the Presence of the Bushmen*, ed. Pippa Skotnes (Cape Town: University of Cape Town Press, 1996), pp. 343–52, and Schrire, *Digging Through Darkness: Chronicles of an Archaeologist* (Charlottesville and London: University Press of Virginia, 1995).

97 *"mindless obstinacy"* · *Journal Général de France*, January 8, 1816.

97 *"his monster vaccinated"* · Ibid. Using Saartjie's death as an opportunity to comment on the virulence of smallpox in the winter of 1816, the piece vaunted Jenner's smallpox vaccine as "the greatest discovery of which medicine may boast."

97 *such a bagatelle* · *Mercure de France* (January 1816), p. 334.

98 *"maladie inflammatoire et éruptive"* · Cuvier, Report on Observations.

98 *Venus decomposing from the pox* · See Emile Zola, *Nana* (Paris: Charpentier, 1880), and as cited in Sander Gilman, "Black Bodies, White Bodies" in *"Race," Writing and Difference*, ed. Henry Louis Gates, Jr. (Chicago: University of Chicago Press, 1986), p. 254.

98 *Zola to Baudelaire, Manet to Picasso* · See Gilman, "Black Bodies, White Bodies," p. 254; Hugh Honour, *The Image of the Black in Western Art*, vol. 4 (Cambridge, Mass.: Harvard University Press, 1989), p. 235; and Jill Matus, "Blonde, Black and Hottentot Venus: Context and Critique in Angela Carter's 'Black Venus,' " *Studies in Short Fiction* 28:4 (Fall 1991), pp. 467–76.

98 *"indulged during her last illness"* · Cuvier, Report on Observations.

98 *"loss for ideal beauty"* · "Varietes," *L'Ambigu*, January 10, 1816, pp. 38–40.

98 *"got hold of the* Venus nigra *"* · Ibid.

98 *the celebrated Hellenistic statue* · For the provenance of the Medici Venus, see Kenneth Clark, *The Nude* (Harmondsworth, Middlesex: Penguin, 1956), p. 370.

99 *in 1802* · See Alistair Horne, *The Seven Ages of Paris: Portrait of a City* (London: Macmillan, 2002) and Hilaire Belloc, *Napoleon* (Hamburg-Paris-Bologna: The Albatross Modern Continental Library, 1933).

99 *no equal* behind · Daniel Lysons, *Collectanea: or a Collection of Advertisements and Paragraphs from Newspapers, Relating to Various Subjects*, vol. Iii, unpublished scrapbook, British Library, p. 106.

99 *Cuvier's private apartments* · Richard Owen, A Report to the Board of Curators of the Museum of the Royal College of Surgeons, Manuscript, Royal College of Surgeons Library and Archives, Lincoln's Inn Fields, London, RCS MS 275, n. 7(3) (1831), p. 8.

99 *"the dirty spirit"* · Ibid., p. 7.

99 *"of the various races"* · Ibid., p. 10.

99 *Stanislas's dwarf* · Joseph-Philippe-François Deleuze, *Histoire et description du Muséum Royal d'Histoire Naturelle* (Paris: M. A. Royer, 1823), p. 660.

99 *"examples of the South American races"* · Ibid.

100 *"privileged visitors"* · Owen, A Report to the Board of Curators of the Royal College of Surgeons, p. 5.

100 *mysteries of creation* · See Mary Shelley, *Frankenstein* (London: Penguin, 1992), p. 49. Mary Shelley began writing Frankenstein in June 1816.

100 *"master of the charnel house"* · Frédéric Cuvier, cited in Dorinda Outram, *Georges Cuvier: Vocation, Science, and Authority in Post-Revolutionary France* (London and Dover, New Hampshire: Manchester University Press, 1984), p. 183. For more on Cuvier's studies, see Anne Fausto-Sterling, "Gender, Race, and Nation: The Comparative Anatomy of 'Hottentot' Women in Europe, 1815–1817," in *Deviant Bodies: Critical Perspectives on Difference in Science and Popular Culture*, eds. Jennifer Terry and Jacqueline Urla (Bloomington & Indianapolis: Indiana University Press, 1995), p. 32.

100 *property of science* · Contemporary commentators who believe that images of Saartjie Baartman should be the preserve only of academic researchers and those who have access to archives should consider carefully this history when seeking to control the circulation of her image. Doubtless some will be shocked or offended by the images; but many people will learn from them. They are part of the story.

100 *Cuvier studied the interiors* · See A. B. Griffiths, *Biographies of Scientific Men* (London: Robert Sutton, 1912), p. 24.

100 *state funeral* · Ibid.

100 *"unusually heavy"* · Franck Bourdier, "Georges Cuvier," *Dictionary of Scientific Biography*, vol. 3, ed. Charles Coulston Gillispie (New York: Charles Scribner's Sons, 1971), p. 524.

100 *"of the lobes"* · Ibid.

101 *"men of note"* · Fausto-Sterling, "Gender, Race, and Nation," p. 44 n. 16.

101 *from the study* · Edward Spitzka, cited in Fausto-Sterling, "Gender, Race, and Nation," p. 44 n. 16.

101 *"all white and all male"* · Stephen Jay Gould, "The Hottentot Venus," *The Flamingo's Smile: Reflections in Natural History* (New York: W. W. Norton and Co., 1985), pp. 291–92.

101 *"la Vénus Hottentote"* · Ibid., p. 292.

101 *"black female sexuality"* · See Gilman, "Black Bodies, White Bodies," pp. 223–61, this reference p. 238.

102 *"than humbly imitate"* · Cited in Schrire, *Digging Through Darkness*, p. 179.

102 *and sextant* · Ibid.

102 *fivefold increase* · Jonathan Thompson, "This year's must have cosmetic surgery: the Beyoncé nip and butt," *The Independent on Sunday*, London, April 17, 2005. The procedure involves implanting bags of silicone, or quantities of fat removed from elsewhere in the body, into the buttocks, and thus making them larger and more pronounced. Ninety percent of people who have the surgery are female.

102 *end results* · See Jonathan Thompson, "This year's must have cosmetic surgery," *The Independent on Sunday*.

102 *would have laughed* · Schrire, *Digging Through Darkness*, p. 183. Schrire's consummate counteranalysis of the history of racist ethnography of the female Khoisan body shows that Khoisan women laughed at the European travelers who bribed or cajoled them to raise their skirts, because showing their genitals was the rudest insult imaginable to their culture—a point the European strangers eternally failed to understand. See Schrire, p. 180.

CHAPTER 11 · LAYING DOWN THE BONES

103 *and the 1850s* · Richard Owen's 1822 report to the Royal College of Surgeons confirms that Saartjie's remains were not yet on public display. No museum record has yet been discovered that confirms the exact date Cuvier's collection went on public display.

103 *from open exhibition* · Phillip V. Tobias, "Saartje Baartman: her life, her remains, and the negotiations for their repatriation from France to South Africa," *South African Journal of Science*, no. 98 (March/April 2002), pp. 107–110.

103 *museum's storerooms* · Stephen Jay Gould, "The Hottentot Venus," *The Flamingo's Smile: Reflections in Natural History* (New York: W. W. Norton & Co., 1985), pp. 291–305, reference p. 291.

104 *1810 and 1815* · Dr. Ben Ngubane, "Efforts to repatriate remains of Saartjie Baartman continue," October 10, 2000, http://www.sabc news.com/Article/0,1093,5652,00.html.

104 *to send back Saartjie's relics* · See Ayesha Ismail, "Victory as Griquas gain first nation status," *Sunday Times* (Cape Town), August 9, 1998, http://www.suntimes.co.za/1998/08/09.news/cape/net07.1; and Resolutions as agreed by Official and Associate Delegates to the National Khoisan Consultative Conference on Khoisan diversity in National Unity held in Oudtshoorn, March 29–April 1, 2001, Urgent Anthropology, http://www.und.ac.za.und/ccms/anthropology/urgent/khoisan.html. In 1997 the Western Cape legislature allocated a grant of R100,000 to Le Fleur's group to cover the costs of Saartjie's repatriation. The same week that the U.N. accorded first nation status to the Khoisan, a delegation representing Khoisan groups met with the Cape legislature to discuss progress on the return of Saartjie's remains, and to plan a campaign for their return.

104 *their rightful owners* · As Ngubane remarked, with pointed irony, so extensive is this plunder that "if all these objects were to be repatriated to South Africa, it would be impossible for them to be properly accommodated, curated and handled within existing facilities." Dr. Ben Ngubane, "Efforts to repatriate remains of Saartjie Baartman continue," October 10, 2000.

104 *"and imperial excesses"* · Tobias, "Saartjie Baartman," p. 109.

104 *share Saartjie's lineage* · See SABC, "Khoi groups claim to be Saartjie's descendents," August 6, 2002, www.sabcnews.com/article/0,1093 ,40207,00; and Zola Maseko and Gail Smith, *The Return of Sarah Baartman*, Black Roots Pictures (Brooklyn, N.Y.: First Run/Icarus Films, 2002).

105 *"in South Africa"* · Cited in Caitlin Davies, *The Return of El Negro: The Compelling Story of Africa's Unknown Soldier* (South Africa: Penguin, 2003), p. 229. During the negotiations, a mystery developed over the whereabouts of Saartjie's viscera. De Lumley claimed they had been accidentally destroyed in the early 1980s. However, in 2002 the museum suddenly, and mysteriously, relocated Saartjie's brain and geni-

tals. These contradictory statements led to later suggestions that the organs returned might not in fact be Saartjie's. See Maseko and Smith, *The Return of Sarah Baartman.*

105 *majority of South Africans* · Interview with Brigitte Mabandla, *Sarah Baartman Funeral,* video footage, August 9, 2002, South African Broadcasting Corporation, 63323-63324.

105 *request for Saartjie* · The nameless "El Negro" was a southern African warrior whose corpse had been grave-robbed in the early nineteenth century by two respected French naturalists. His stuffed body and personal effects finally ended up in a museum in the small Spanish town of Bagnoles. Following a decade of protest and diplomacy, Spain agreed to return El Negro to Botswana in 2000. See Davies, *The Return of El Negro.*

105 *"colonialism, and racism"* · SABC, "Hottentot Venus may finally come home," January 28, 2002, http://www.sabcnews.com/article/0,1093,27402,00.html.

106 *"as an African"* · Ibid.

106 *"the true monstrosity"* · Cited in Chris McGreal, "Coming Home," *The Guardian* (London), February 21, 2002, http://education.guardian.co.uk/0,3858,4360082.00.html.

106 *Khoisan descent* · Diana Ferrus; eds. Malika Coming Ndlovu, Deela Khan, Shelley Barry, *Ink@Boilingpoint: A Selection of 21st Century Black Women's Writing from the Tip of Africa* (Cape Town: WEAVE Collective, 2002). The poem promises to bring Saartjie home:

> *I have come to wrench you away—*
> *away from the poking eyes*
> *of the man-made monster*
> *who lives in the dark*
> *with his clutches of imperialism*
> *who dissects your body bit by bit*
> *who likens your soul to that of Satan*
> *and declares himself the ultimate god!*

106 *"to all our people"* · Maseko and Smith, *The Return of Sarah Baartman.*

107 *"in the sunset"* · Thabo Mbeki, "Speech at the Funeral of Sarah Baart-

man," Hankey, South Africa, August 9, 2002, www.anc.org.za/anc
docs/history/mbeki/2002/tm0809.html.

107 *for burial* · SABC, "Saartjie Baartman to be enrobed," August 3, 2002,
http://sabcnews.com/article/0,1093,39990,00.html.

107 *"the nation's grandmother"* · Maseko and Smith, *The Return of Sarah
Baartman.*

107 *solve the question* · Jackson Zweliyanyikima Vena at the Cory Library for
Historical Research, University of Rhodes, is currently engaged in genealogical research in the Eastern Cape. I am grateful to him for
sharing his knowledge on Saartjie's Eastern Cape origins, and his observations on the significance of her traditional burial rites.

107 *divided racial groups* · Willa Boezak summed it up: "[When] we celebrate her homecoming it will be a spiritual ceremony. It will be a re-
burial. It will not be a Cape Town thing, it will not be a Griqua thing,
it will be a national thing." Willa Boezak, cited in Caroline Hooper-
Box, "Baartman Set for Return to African Soil," *The Sunday Independent,* South Africa, February 2, 2002, and see www.int.iol.co.za.

108 *her dignity* · In parliament, African National Congress MP Nosipho
Ntwanambi condemned Saartjie's exploitation and welcomed the
restoration of her dignity. The burial of her remains, Ntwanambi
said, "would reflect the new non-racial and respectful South Africa."
Bridget Mabandla made a forceful demand in parliament for "the
continuation of the struggle and for the ultimate emancipation of
women." SABC, "Inhumane suffering of Sarah Barmann condemned," August 7, 2002, http://sabcnews.com/article/0,1093
,40280,00.

108 *rallies and demonstrations* · On the day of Saartjie's funeral, the Commission for Gender Equality organized a march in Pretoria to com-
memorate the 1956 women's demonstrations against the pass laws.
The march remembered the women persecuted during the struggle
against apartheid, and celebrated their achievements. Honoring
Saartjie in their speeches, the protesters acknowledged the government's successes in addressing gender issues since 1994. However,
they pointed out that there was still a great deal of work to be done,
especially in tackling high rates of rape and abuse of women and children.

108 *named after her* · The Saartjie Baartman Centre, located in Athlone, a
township near Cape Town. Academic Yvette Abrahams said, "Women
visiting here must be able to say I went to Sarah Bartmann and she
gave me shelter. What makes me proud is the way she lives in people's
lives." SABC, "Sarah Bartmann celebrated," August 7, 2002, http:
//sabcnews.com/article/1,093,40224,00.html.

108 *thousand people* · Press reports suggested seven thousand attended the
funeral. Judging from estimates of people who were there, and film
coverage, two to three thousand is a more accurate number.

108 *all these years* · *Sarah Baartman Funeral,* August 9, 2002, South African
Broadcasting Corporation, 63323-63324.

109 *"somewhere in Europe"* · Ibid.

109 *"in our own past"* · Ibid.

109 *Thabo Mbeki's speech* · This, and all subsequent references from Thabo
Mbeki's speech, are from Mbeki, "Speech at the Funeral of Sarah
Baartman."

110 *"carnal curiosity"* · Neville Hoad, "Thabo Mbeki's AIDS Blues: The Intellectual, The Archive, and the Pandemic," *Public Culture* 17(1), pp.
101–128, especially p. 108 (Durham, N.C.: Duke University Press,
2005).

110 *"bordering on criminality"* · Dr. Mamphele Ramphele, 13th International AIDS Conference, Durban, South Africa, July 2000.

111 *HIV/AIDS* · For the most comprehensive analysis of how Mbeki used
the occasion of his speech at Saartjie's funeral to make a position
statement on HIV/AIDS, see Hoad, "Thabo Mbeki's AIDS Blues,"
Public Culture, pp. 101–127. As Mbeki stood at Saartjie's graveside
championing women's rights, his government was engaged in a
fierce, landmark court battle to prevent HIV-positive women from ac-
cessing a lifesaving drug, Nevirapine, proven to dramatically reduce
the risk of mother-to-child transmission of the HIV virus. Mbeki
stated, "It will never be possible for us to claim that we are making significant progress to create a new South Africa if we do not make significant progress towards gender equality and the emancipation of
women." Yet as he spoke, his government ignored the raised voices of
hundreds of thousands of women who demanded the right to treat-
ments that would save the lives of their children. For a full account
and legal and medical analysis of the MTCT case, its attendant issues

and broader political implications, see Mark Heywood, "Preventing
Mother-to-Child HIV Transmission in South Africa: Background,
Strategies and Outcomes of the Treatment Action Campaign Case
Against the Minister of Health," *South African Journal of Human Rights*
19 (2003), pp. 278–315. Further documentation relating to the case
is also available at www.tac.org.za.

AFTERLIFE

112 *"of its truth"* · Cited in Iain Bamforth, ed., *The Body in the Library: A Literary Anthology of Modern Medicine* (London: Verso, 2003), p. ix.

112 *"dark continent"* · Sigmund Freud, "The Question of Lay Analysis"
(1926), in *The Standard Edition of the Complete Psychological Works*, eds.
James Strachey and Anna Freud (London: Hogarth, 1953–74), vol.
20 (1959).

113 *admissibly human* · Felipe Fernandez-Armesto, *So You Think You're
Human? A Brief History of Mankind* (Oxford: Oxford University Press,
2004), p. 84.

113 *"among humans"* · Ibid., p. 89.

113 *"referring to . . . groups"* · Caitlin Davies, *The Return of El Negro: The Compelling Story of Africa's Unknown Soldier* (South Africa: Penguin, 2003),
p. 52.

113 *"than their differences"* · Ibid.

114 *life demonstrates* · Thirty years later, the discovery of mitochondrial
DNA (mtDNA) made it possible to work out the relatedness among
different populations of people, and to date when their ancestors di-
verged. Mitochondria are energy-producing cell configurations
coded with their own DNA, containing only the mother's line. Studies analyzing mtDNA have now concluded that modern humans
began in Africa, probably just south of the Sahara desert. Somewhere
in the region, that is, originally inhabited by the Khoisan.

114 *"of our country"* · *Sarah Baartman Funeral*, August 9, 2002, South
African Broadcasting Corporation, 63323-63324.

114 *will of others* · Thabo Mbeki, "Speech at the Funeral of Sarah Baartman," Hankey, South Africa, August 9, 2002, www.anc.za/ancdocs
/history/mbeki/2002/tm0809.html. She was used, Mbeki reminded
mourners, to prove "the alleged promiscuity of the African women

who, it was claimed, invited either man or ape. . . . Sarah Baartman was taken to Europe to tell this lie in the most dramatic way possible. She was ferried to Europe as an example of the sexual depravity and the incapacity to think of the African woman in the first instance and the African in general. The legacy of those centuries remains with us, both in the way in which our society is structured and in the ideas that many in our country continue to carry in their heads, which inform their reaction on important matters." One of these psychological legacies is a suspicion of Western science and medicine, used in previous ages to implement, justify, and enforce racism; a legacy that Mbeki's speech attempted to use as validation for his government's refusal to adequately fulfill its democratic responsibility to provide lifesaving medicines and treatment for those with HIV and AIDS in South Africa.

114 *"a cipher, a perfect victim"* · Toni Morrison, *Playing in the Dark: Whiteness and the Literary Imagination* (Cambridge, Mass.: Harvard University Press, 1992), p. 24.

115 *by her grave* · Makhumandile "Trompies" Bantom had been kidnapped and murdered for his R150,000 inheritance by Ayanda Kwinana, now serving a life sentence.

115 *made in Holland* · The *Sarah Baartman* is the flagship of a series of four patrol vessels named after women whose names are synonymous with the struggle for freedom and the restoration of dignity for South African people. The other three ships, *Lilian Ngoyi, Ruth First,* and *Victoria Mxenge,* are named after freedom fighters against tyranny. Saartjie's inclusion as a historical grandmother among these great twentieth-century leaders testifies to her cultural and political status in contemporary South Africa.

INDEX

About the Author

Writer, critic, and broadcaster, RACHEL HOLMES is the
author of *Scanty Particulars* (2003), the biography of
Dr. James Barry, and a former professor of English at
the University of London and the University of Sussex.
She lives in London and Cape Town.